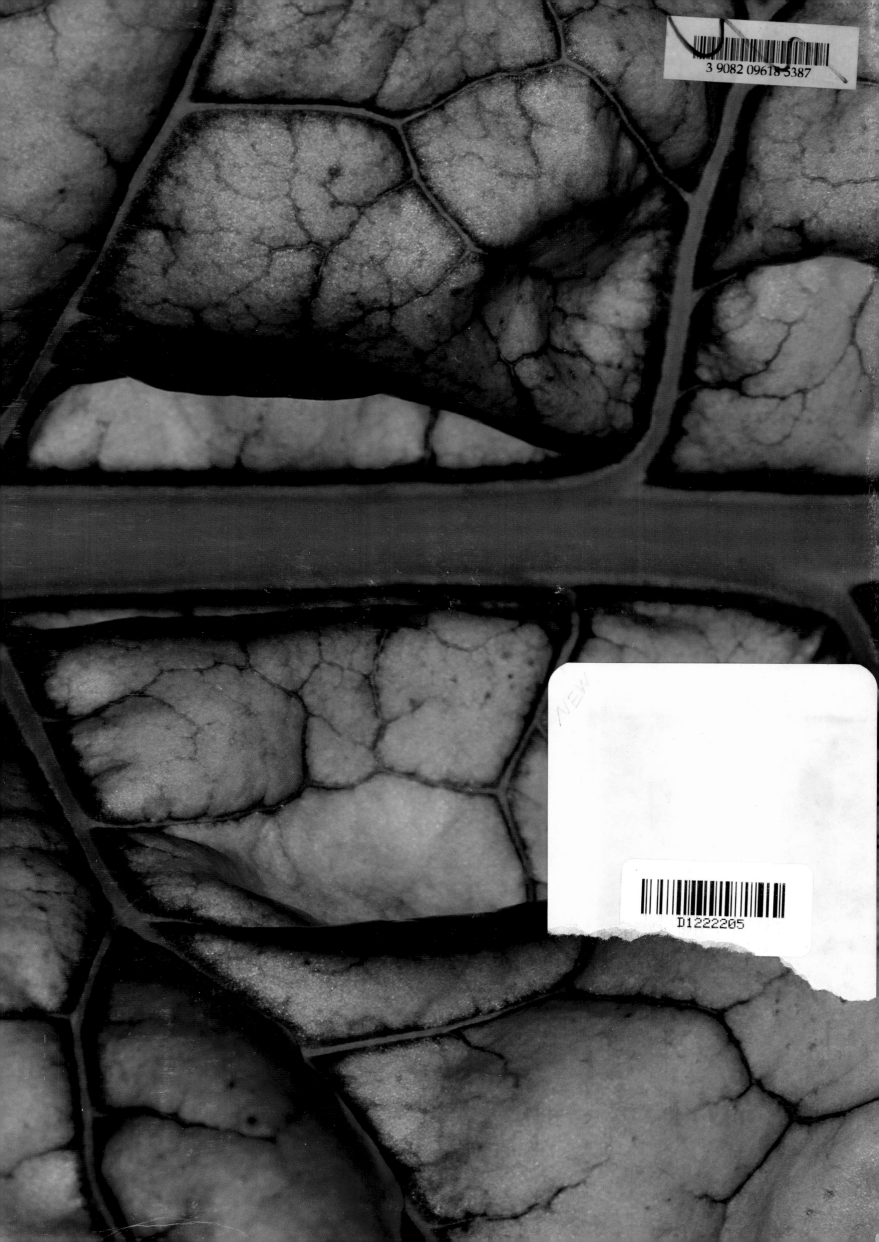

kitchen garden

A to Z

Growing
Harvesting
Buying
Storing

Text by Mike McGrath
Photography by Gordon Smith

Harry N. Abrams, Inc., Publishers

Contents

Introduction

Kitchen gardens grow much more than food.

My wife's fondest childhood memories are of visits to her grand-parents' "farm" in summer: endless rows of tomato and pepper plants, fresh peas and onions, and—most important to her personally—a giant raspberry patch where she would spend the afternoon pretending to pick, only to return to the house with a red-stained face and an empty bucket.

Thanks to those memories, what she wanted most when we got our first house was a big garden surrounded by raspberries.

It wasn't much in the beginning—a few raised beds filled mostly with tomatoes and enough canes to provide a couple of pints of fresh berries. Over the years, more beds were built, more crops were added, and the raspberries did not so much flourish as threaten. The canes reproduced so prolifically and geometrically that a fresh pint a day quickly became the in-season norm. Then a quart. Then a gallon. Then gallons.

Herbs and garlic made a welcome entrance. And once enough beds had been built to grow all the tomatoes we would need for a full year, flowers—edible and "just for nice"—muscled their pretty way in. We experienced the thrill of horticultural victory with the matchless, intensely floral taste of alpine strawberries grown from seed; the agony of defeat when flea beetles shotgunned the eggplant.

When all the available ground was finally filled up, big pots and other containers came into play, bringing herbs and hot peppers closer to the kitchen and another dimension of display and color to the garden. More and more flowers flourished in what had once been just an exercise for eating: Peas grew close to pansies by the front door; canna lilies popped up next to lettuces; spinach shared space with salvia in the front flower beds. And now we had so many raspberries that friends were begged to come and pick as many of the sweet treats as they could.

. . . Then we learned from older family members that the grandparents who were responsible for all this bounty hadn't lived on a farm; they had simply filled all the available space around their single home with garden areas. Our plots are probably very close in size to the ones they so lovingly tended. The wonderful haze of memory had exaggerated the space by acres—but not the taste of the fruits that grew there.

Our children will probably make this garden bigger when they remember going out to pick raspberries when they were small, returning with empty buckets and red-stained faces.

With any luck, so will their children.

Kitchen gardens grow so much more than food.

Build a memory this spring.

—Mike McGrath, at the time of pea-planting, 2004

1. Simply raising your growing area higher than the surrounding soil provides a wealth of benefits, thanks to the looser earth and improved drainage of such raised beds. The untreated regular old wood boards used here for frames will last for years.

2. Oregano and flowers share a warming bed of stone.

3. Lack of space is an issue in most gardens, but do not skimp on the width of your walking lanes. They will seem to shrink over the summer—as large plants "lean" into them—so make them nice and big to begin with.

Opposite page: Stone beds do not need to be laid out in straight lines; such materials are at their best when allowed to curve into a more naturalistic design. This winding bed makes for a very calming garden element. Many of the beds in my garden are framed with stone unearthed during the building process. The one second from the top is made of Novawood, from Obex—this woodlike material lasts forever and is made completely from otherwise impossible-to-recycle (uncoded) plastics. The frames above and below it are made of Trex, a wood and plastic composite.

One of the easiest ways to maintain a happy, healthy, productive garden is to raise your growing beds above the surrounding soil line. Raised beds warm up faster and drain better than flat ground gardens; provide protection against floods; and insure a loose, "friable" earth by creating a visible barrier against the intrusion of soil-compacting feet.

Raised beds can be any length, but should always be four feet wide; this provides the maximum growing space while still allowing you to reach the center of the bed from either side without stepping on the raised area. The lanes (walking areas) between the beds must be *at least* two feet wide; towering plants will encroach on these paths greatly by midsummer.

Map out your design, then use a garden fork (see page 28) to loosen up the soil in the areas that will become the beds. Then shovel soil from the areas that will become your walking lanes up onto the beds until the raised areas are six inches to a foot higher than the lanes. The loose soil that now graces those beds is very conducive to healthy plant growth. *Never* step into your raised beds; always work with your feet outside their earth.

UNFRAMED BEDS: In the French Intensive System, raised beds slope naturally to form mounds. This method provides as much as 20 percent extra growing room when smallish plants such as alpine strawberries, lettuces, and compact flowers adorn the sides.

FRAMED BEDS: Framing your beds provides a more formal structure and greater protection during floods. Any nontoxic material can be used. Among the most popular choices are:

WOOD: Cedar, redwood, locust, and Osage orange are naturally rot resistant. Many gardeners simply frame their beds with inexpensive "regular" wood, which will survive for many years and return its nutrients to the earth when it finally does decay. Never use pressure-treated wood or railroad ties.

STONE: Many gardens-to-be are filled with rocks and fieldstone. Rather than haul this native material away, use it to frame your beds. The look is very attractive, and stone frames extend the growing season by absorbing heat during the day and radiating it back into the soil at night.

PLASTIC: Trex is a mixture of recycled plastic and wood shavings formed into products that include deck flooring and faux landscape timbers; it looks like wood, can be worked like wood, and will last virtually forever. 100 percent recycled plastic products, like Novawood from the Obex Corporation, are equally long-lasting wood look-alikes that often come in kits that fit together like big Lincoln Logs.

In the wild, plants are fed naturally—by fallen leaves, decayed trees, and manure from birds and animals. Such humble fertilizers have nurtured every plant that exists today—the giant sequoias, the grasses of the Great Plains, the hardwood forests of the North, and wildflower fields everywhere. We imitate this magnificent system when we make compost.

One inch of finished compost a year is all the food most plants require. Compost also improves soil structure, adds organic matter, and prevents plant disease better than any chemical fungicide. Spread it around established plants, dig it into new beds, or place some in a porous cloth container in cool water for 24 hours and use the resulting "compost tea" as the perfect liquid fertilizer. (See "Feeding," pages 38–39.)

The best compost is made by combining shredded "dry brown" carbon-rich materials like fall leaves with "wet green" nitrogen-rich components like nonmeat kitchen waste, dried clippings from herbicide-free lawns, spent garden plants, and barnyard manures. Microorganisms in the dry browns feed on the nitrogen in the green matter, creating the rich, crumbly, soil-like compost gardeners call "black gold."

THE COLD HEAP: "If you pile it, it will rot." Over the course of a year or more, piled raw ingredients will slowly become compost. A good plant food and soil conditioner, this compost will not prevent plant diseases.

HOT COMPOST: By mixing approximately four parts shredded leaves to one part wet green material in a system that allows for airflow, heat is generated and composting occurs *much* more rapidly. A superior plant food and superb disease fighter, this compost teems with beneficial organisms that enhance soil life. Hot compost can be made in a classic cedarwood slatted bin, a "cage" of animal fencing, or any other nontoxic container with numerous openings for airflow. To move things along even faster, add a handful of finished compost to every new pile.

1. The classic wooden slatted Lehigh-style cedar compost bin. The cedar is naturally rot-resistant and the open areas between the slats allow for beneficial airflow; the more air, the faster raw ingredients will become compost.

2. A trade-off. Stationary units like this recycled plastic Earth Machine lack airflow and can take quite a while to create their "black gold." But the convenient door at the bottom provides easy access to the material that is always ready first, no matter the system.

3. Spinners like this Green Magic device provide compost *and* aerobic exercise; you turn these "giant trash cans on a spindle" end over end manually to mix the contents—and build up those arm and shoulder muscles.

Opposite page: An inch of compost applied to the top of the soil is all the food this lovely lettuce will require.

Gardeners have been endlessly fascinated by the legendary planting combinations—garlic and roses; marigolds and *anything*—that purportedly insure the success of at least one of the plants involved. The truth of companion planting is even more fascinating than the lore. It *is* a valuable technique that increases the vigor of the plants involved. And it *is* one of a gardener's best defenses against pests and disease. But no "magical combinations" need apply.

True companion planting works on several levels. The first is *structural;* for instance, planning your garden so that the final spring runs of heat-shy lettuce and spinach will be shaded by a tall crop, like sweet corn—keeping their soil cooler and allowing the greens to survive much longer as the weather gets hotter. Another is *nutritional,* where crops with very different food needs follow each other in succession—a fall planting of nitrogen-hungry root crops like potatoes or garlic following phosphorus- and potassium-loving flowering plants like tomatoes or zucchini, for instance—to avoid depleting specific soil nutrients. Another is *beneficial;* positioning plants that produce abundant small flowers, like herbs, near crops that tend to suffer insect attack in your garden; the nectar and pollen in the tiny flowers attract beneficial insects like ladybugs and lacewings—whose *main* diet is troublesome pests.

But the biggest benefit of companion planting is much more general. Simply cultivating a "mixed garden" whenever possible will greatly increase your yields and decrease your problems. As you can well imagine, if you group all your tomatoes in one spot, any disease or insect that gets a foothold will rampage through the other plants very quickly. But if you have only a single tomato plant in the center of each of your raised beds, a problem that occurs on one plant cannot immediately spread to the rest.

1. Sorry, but these marigolds do *not* deserve their legendary reputation for repelling pests in companion planting systems. Slugs and rabbits actually enjoy them quite a bit. But their presence among vegetables does lure pollinating insects, thus insuring a larger bounty of flowers and food for all. In the South, plowing them under deters root knot nematodes.

2. A wonderful combination—tricolor sage, onions, and edible flowers—an herb, a root crop, and a salad adornment. Such a mix is much safer from insect and disease attack than just a bed of any of the individual occupants.

3. Broccoli and flowers share a bed. Do not look for magic combinations, just mix, mix, mix, and all will be well.

Opposite page: Marigolds, Ordono hot peppers, and kale.

The secret to a having an easy-care, healthy garden is to invite in as many kinds of living creatures as you possibly can. Provide multiple water sources, lots of flowering plants, avoid toxic pesticides (which wipe out *many* more friends than foes), and your garden will be well protected and pollinated by the life you invite.

Birds are very reliable garden protectors. Some, like black-capped chickadees and swallows, eat insects exclusively. But in the spring, virtually all birds, including those that are seed eaters the rest of the year, join in the feast—they need the extra protein to raise their young.

Toads and *frogs* are pest-control champions—they eat enormous numbers of insects, the vast majority of them garden pests.

Ladybugs. Everyone loves the "ladies." But how would you react to the sight of small, dragon-shaped, alligator-like creatures on your prized plants? It should be with joy, as these are the ladybugs' larval form, which dine exclusively on soft-bodied pests. Similar in appearance is the larval form of the diaphanous *lacewing,* whose babies are so ferocious in appetite that their common name is "the aphid lion."

The *praying mantis* is a well-known pest predator, welcome in every garden. But wise gardeners treasure *spiders* even more; these stalwart protectors eat huge numbers of insects that would otherwise threaten your plants—and garden spiders do not bother people or pets. Scatter small piles of straw throughout the garden to attract them in the spring.

Wasps. Braconid, *Trichogramma,* and other species of almost invisible *predator wasps* parasitize pest caterpillars like the tomato hornworm, covering them with egg cases that look like natural spines. Regular-size wasps take care of such business the old-fashioned way—using their large wings to carry the pests away.

Bees, especially native species, are essential pollinators of many food crops and flowers. And these buzzing flower fulfillers pose little to no stinging threat to people; the only such insect that does is the yellowjacket, a nonpollinating wasp, not a bee.

1. The presence of this turtle is a clear indicator that the garden is organic and teeming with life.

2. Toads and frogs are some of the finest garden protectors, often eating their own weight in bad bugs every day.

3. Never "import" praying mantises into your garden; it disrupts the natural order. When native species arrive on their own, however, encourage them to stay.

4. Those are not natural spines on that destructive tomato hornworm's back. They are the egg cases of a beneficial wasp so tiny we can barely see it. Leave it alone; it will soon give birth to a legion of tiny exterminators.

Opposite page: A birdbath in the center of your garden will cut your pest problems in half.

A weed, they say, is a wonderful plant growing in the wrong place. That first part is often very true. Harvest the distinctive sawtoothed leaves of dandelions when they are *very* young (*before* any flower buds form) and add to salads for a delicious and healthful spring tonic—then dispatch the rest of the "crop" with a no-bend root-popper tool before they can set seed.

Of course, not all weeds are so useful. The best way to control the rest is to prevent them with mulch. A greatly misused term, "mulch" refers to any substance used to cover the soil to prevent weeds and retain moisture. Compost is *not* mulch—it feeds plants and prevents disease, but does not keep moisture in the soil or deter unwanted plants.

Shredded fall leaves make the best mulch; an inch-thick layer will deter any weed and keep moisture in the soil wonderfully, lessening the need to water during dry times. Earthworms also love to live under such leaf litter, and their castings are a perfect food your plants will greatly enjoy. But shredded your leaves *must* be; whole ones mat down and prevent the passage of air and water.

Dried clippings from an herbicide-free lawn have been found to suppress weeds better than black plastic. To prevent matting, allow the clippings to air-dry for 24 hours before applying an inch-thick layer around your plants.

The best store-bought mulch is *straw.* Just be sure you get straw and not hay. A straw bale consists of tightly packed hollow plant *stems* (like drinking straws). A bale of hay, on the other hand, is meant to feed livestock; its grain heads create weedy nightmares in gardens. (Trust your eyes, not signage, to tell them apart—too many people use the terms interchangeably.)

Do *not* use wood chips, shavings, shredded bark, or sawdust. Wood mulches suck nitrogen out of the soil, often starving the plants they were intended to protect. They *can* be used safely to prevent weeds in nonplanted areas, such as the lanes between raised beds. (But do not use within 30 feet of a home or a car—the "shotgun" or "artillery" fungi that breed in such mulches can permanently stain nearby surfaces.)

1. Grass clippings from an herbicide-free lawn are the most weed-suppressive garden mulch. Collect the clippings, let them dry for a day, then apply an inch-thick layer around your plants.

2. Straw is the best garden mulch you can purchase; one bale goes a long way. Just make sure you get straw, not hay—whose seed heads would turn your garden into amber waves of grain.

3. The Weed Hound is one of several tools that can pop dandelions out of the ground while you stand up straight.

Opposite page: An inch-thick layer of shredded leaves will protect this broccoli against drought and weeds.

Given a big enough "pot," you can grow anything in a container you could in bare ground. And, unlike plants in bare ground, containers can be moved around to cover the occasional garden imperfection or switched for a different effect.

Containers can be metal, plastic, glass, wood—any material that is not toxic (do *not* use railroad ties, pressure-treated wood, or cans that held gasoline, paint, oil, chemicals or the like). Do *not* think small; larger is almost always better. Imagine the final size of the plant before you commit any container to a specific use.

Drainage is crucial. Most containers designed for planting should already have drainage holes. But never assume—and always check the bottom for plugs that need to be removed before using. Water *must* be able to drain out freely—if the drainage holes are flush with the ground, prop the container up with bricks or other supports that allow easy egress. Saucers underneath containers are fine for protecting surfaces, but water should never be left standing in them.

WARNING: *Many* more containerized plants are lost to overwatering and/or inadequate drainage than to all other causes combined.

Never use garden soil to fill containers. Outdoors, plants make up for less-than-perfect soil by sending roots out great distances in search of water and food; they cannot do this in containers, where physics compresses those heavy garden soils even more.

The perfect container mixture is a combination of one part compost for substance and nutrition, and three parts of a "soil-less" or "soil-free" mixture for lightness and drainage. "Soil-free" mixtures are available at any garden center or nursery, but beware of the words "potting soil" on a label; such bags often contain worse dirt than your garden and are better suited for *making* clay pots than for filling them. Reject bags that feel heavy; the right mix will seem almost impossibly light for its size (mixtures labeled "for seed starting" are almost always a good bet).

1. Strawberry pots are well named. Although you could fill their little "windows" with many different plants, berries—like these alpines—enjoy growing high above the slugs and ground rots they must normally endure.

2. This lemon balm looks wonderful in its big metal container, and can be easily moved to wherever homeowners and guests might need quick protection from mosquitoes. More important, the solid metal will restrain the invasive herb from annexing nearby garden beds.

3. This cut-and-come-again container of lettuce can sit right outside the kitchen door.

Opposite page: Sage in concrete.

Most premixed "soil free" mediums are largely peat, with perlite and/or vermiculite, some compost or "composted forest products," and a bit of lime to level out the pH. Those ingredients are all fine. But read the labels carefully: some mixes also contain chemical fertilizer (avoid these types), water-holding crystals (your choice; the crystals supposedly help stretch the time between waterings, but I have not found them to make a difference), and/or plant-friendly mycorrhizal bacteria (very beneficial—they bring soil life to the party).

If you use a clean premixed formula (like Fafard or Pro-Mix), add some compost (yours, another gardener's, bulk from a nursery, or a bagged product); three parts soil-free mix to one part compost. This adds substance, feeds your container's contents naturally, and introduces essential life to the planting medium.

Or create your own custom mixture. In a wheelbarrow or large tub, combine equal amounts of peat, compost, and perlite and/or vermiculite. (See below for a discussion of these ingredients individually.) Continually moisten the mixture as you combine the ingredients and then use it to fill your containers. Do *not* put rocks, potshards, or similar materials into the bottom of your containers—they will not improve the drainage but *will* take up valuable root space. Instead, lay down screening in the bottom to prevent any of your mix from coming out of the drainage holes.

CAUTION: Soil-free mixes and their individual ingredients are light and dusty; moisten your materials thoroughly and wear a dust mask when working.

PEAT: The "milled peat moss" available in large bricks at virtually all garden centers, not "whole" sphagnum moss. Extraordinarily light in weight, peat holds moisture excellently *and* drains well. Its natural antibiotic activity also prevents mold from forming. Like the bogs it comes from, peat is highly acidic, so add a tablespoon of lime or wood ash for every five gallons of mix to balance the pH. *Coir,* a similar substance made from coconut husks, can be substituted for peat.

PERLITE: Those little round white balls in planting and potting mixes are not foam or plastic; they are a completely natural mined mineral "popped" by heat into a sphere. Perlite enhances drainage, improves airflow to root systems, and makes containers more lightweight and easy to move.

VERMICULITE: Although it looks like shavings from the back of a mirror, this is another mined, "popped" mineral. Vermiculite, like perlite, is also lightweight and drains well—but its very different physical structure adds more "substance" to a container mix. Note: Some samples of vermiculite have been found to contain small traces of asbestos fibers (naturally present in the original mined ores). If this concerns you, simply use more perlite instead.

1. Mix equal amounts of the individual components—peat (left), perlite (bottom), compost (right), and vermiculite (top)—together, moistening the mix as you work to keep the dust down.

2. Fill your containers completely with the mixture. No rocks or potshards in the bottom; your plants prefer soil down there.

3. Then carefully place your plants in the container. Do not overcrowd them—think of how big they will be mid-season and plan for their size *then*—not for the tiny little things you are looking at now.

Opposite page: A potpourri of pots. Note the full-grown basil plants from photo 3 above front and center.

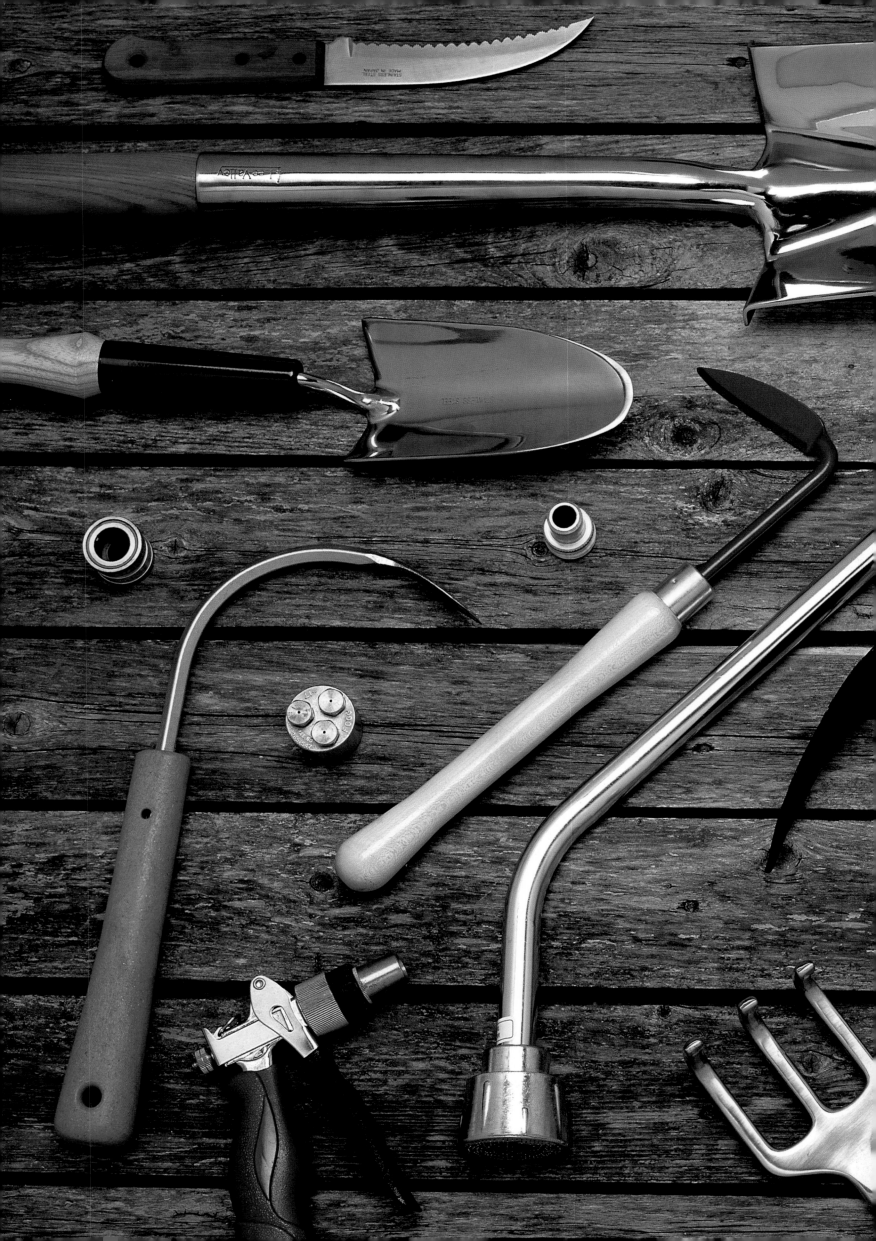

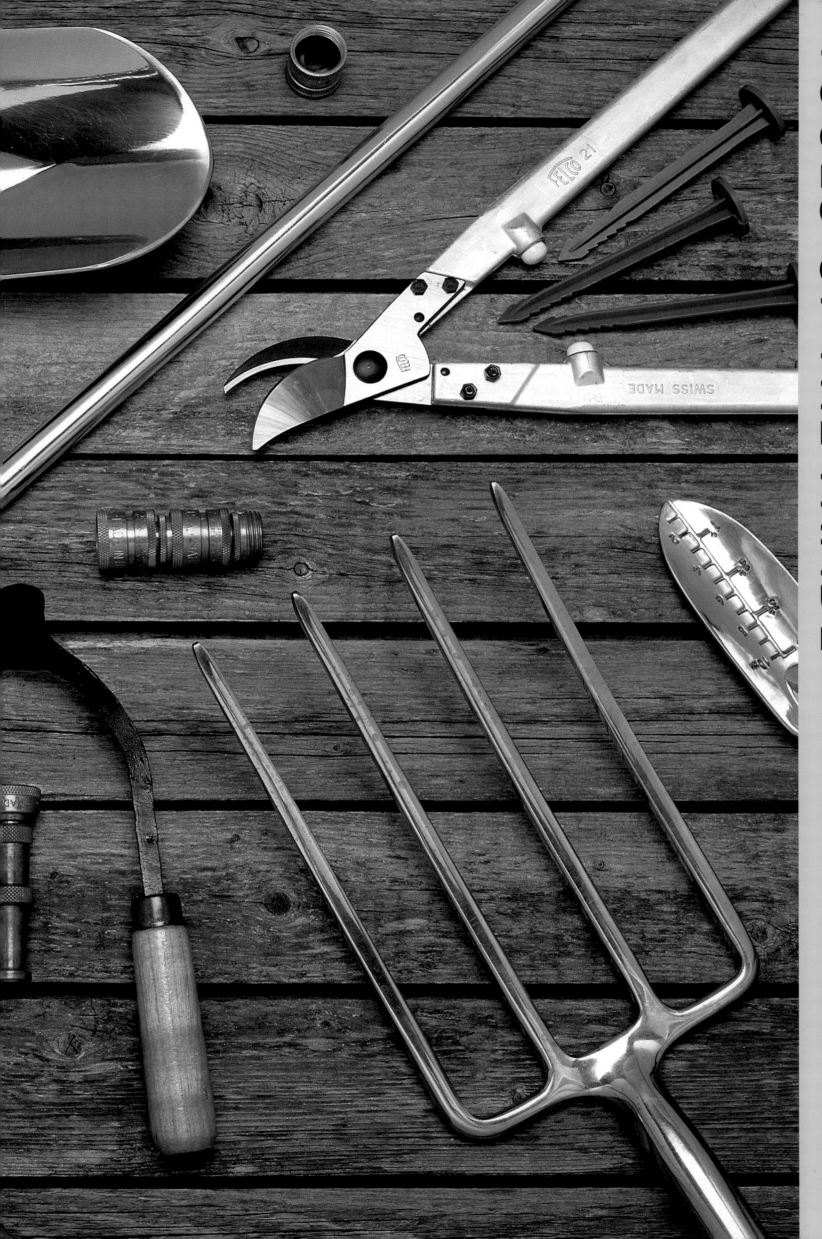

You may need a shovel to get started, but after that, hoes will see your garden through to success. Perhaps the most ancient of the dedicated gardening tools, hoes can be used roughly to clear an area of ground, delicately to smooth out the surface for planting, and then to slice efficiently below the soil line to dispatch any weeds during the growing season. Some hoes are generalists that perform all these functions, but many have abandoned the clearing of ground and smoothing-out functions to concentrate on more efficient and specialized weed removal.

There are almost as many styles of hoes as there are gardeners—from the ancient "flat-heads on long handles" that worked the soils of ancient Roman vineyards to clever new inventions whose blades are shaped like discs and bats. The style of a hoe's bladehead is very important to the task at hand, but from the gardener's perspective, the length of the shaft and the feel of the tool are equally crucial.

A hoe should be of a length that allows you to work the soil without bending over or down. It should feel comfortable in your hands. It must be light enough for you to use for an hour without exhausting your arms, but weighty enough to defeat weeds with one pass. Hoes with fiberglass shafts will be lighter than wooden ones, but also more flexible, which may work against the gardener in heavy soils. Taller gardeners should seek out hoes with longer handles and "gooseneck" or "swan's neck" designs, where the head is angled back toward the user.

Take the time to insure comfort before you buy. Do not be shy about trying out different types in the store for feel and length. Experiment with other people's hoes to see which style works best for you. Each gardener is unique, and there is no best hoe for everyone. But there *is* one for you, and finding it is one of the true triumphs of gardening. (Mine is an Australian model with an exceptionally long handle and a head shaped like the Bat-Signal.) Always keep the blades of your hoes sharp.

THE DIAMOND HOE: Sharp all around and small enough to get into tight spaces, this tool is designed to dispatch weeds on both the pushing and pulling motions, thus spreading the work to different muscles during a long day of weeding.

THE ITALIAN HOE: The oldest-known design, in use for millennia. Also known as the grape hoe, grub hoe, draw hoe, and, in California, by many Italians fondly as the Dago hoe in honor of the ancestors who brought it—and their inspiring gardening traditions—to our shores. If the head is welded on (as opposed to the traditional Italian design where the shaft runs through a round slot that is part of the top of the bladehead), call it an American, standard, or shank hoe. No matter the name, the wide, flat head is unsurpassed at clearing weedy areas, smoothing out soil, and cultivating between wide rows.

1. The American, or "standard," version of the Italian hoe. The original has a heavier metal head that includes a socket above the blade for the shaft, and is unparalled at chopping up poor soil. This modified version is much lighter and easier to use for long periods of time.

2. The diamond hoe, sharp all around the head. Two big advantages to the diamond design: The small head can reach into very tight spaces, and the tool cuts on both the back and forth motions.

3. The oddly angled head of the collinear hoe keeps it tightly parallel to the ground. Because, as Willie Sutton might note, that's where the weeds are. Most hoe heads are bladed on only one side, but the collinear's sharp-all-around design allows it to take out weeds on both the push and pull strokes.

4. The Winged Weeder; standard head, short-handled version. Winged Weeder heads come in this (8-inch) width and a smaller-headed version half this size that is especially good for precision weeding.

5. The Ho Mi weeder. A modern tool based on an ancient design, its somewhat primitive look disguises surprisingly ergonomic aspects that allow you to chop tough weeds out of soil for long periods without fatigue.

THE COLLINEAR HOE: Not designed for rough work, the small, very sharp, uniquely angled, parallel-to-the-ground blade makes this a tool of choice for removing weeds in tight places and for making exceedingly level planting beds. Its light weight and ease of use are popular with gardeners whose arm strength or endurance is limited.

THE WINGED WEEDER: One of the best of the "new design" hoes. The head of the original Winged Weeder is an eight-inch-wide triangle, sharp on all sides. It would be *the* perfect tool for cultivating between too-tight rows if not for the Winged Weeder Junior, whose blade is only half as wide. "Junior's" head may look humorously small on a regular-length shaft, but the weeds are not laughing. The combination of a very small, very sharp bladehead on a long shaft allows gardeners to dispatch weeds growing right next to wanted plants from quite a distance. Both size heads are also available on short handles for close-up precision weeding.

THE STIRRUP HOE: So called because it looks much like the stirrup on a saddle, this is also called the oscillating, hula, or action hoe. The unique open-style blade rests on a pivot, so that the head rocks as you move it back and forth in the soil, uprooting many different types of troublesome weeds in one stroke. It is also very useful for true cultivation—that is, the breaking up and aerating of hard, crusty soil.

THE SCUFFLE HOE: Sharp on the front and toothed on the back; it cuts weeds down with the blade and then "picks" them up with those teeth.

THE WARREN HOE: Also known as the onion hoe, this tool is a nineteenth-century precursor of the Winged Weeder, but with a heavier, more three-dimensional head angled backward (the "gooseneck" design) toward the user. Good for weeding in tight spaces, it is the perfect tool for carving out straight rows for direct seeding of crops like beans and peas.

CULTIVATORS: Many gardeners use these as hoes (they are sometimes called potato hoes, as they were originally designed for harvesting that underground crop). Available in a variety of sizes, the claw-shaped heads can have three, four, or five tines and are excellent tools for stirring soil, either to break up a crusty surface or to dispatch tender young weeds.

HO MI: One of the most popular of the "new design" weeders (actually said to be an ancient tool from Asia) is the oddly angled Ho Mi; its sharp, broad blade is designed to slide easily underneath weeds like dandelions, whose long taproots defy other tools.

Although many suppliers (and gardeners) use the terms interchangeably, there are differences. Shovels tend to have broader heads and are used to break ground, dig large holes, and move ("shovel") items like snow, coal, and manure. Spades are generally shorter in length and have either sharp, somewhat flattened heads (border spades) for edging work, or elongated heads (poaching spades) for digging small holes and popping plants out of the ground. Do not worry about names; choose the tool that best fits your height, strength, and needs.

SHAFTS: Fiberglass is lighter and preferable for light work, especially of long duration in loose soils. The extra weight of a solid wood shaft lends heft and strength to hard jobs and heavy soils—and many gardeners simply prefer the feel. Like baseball bats, the best wooden shafts are made of ash or hickory. A true handle (in the shape of a D when seen from the side) adds welcome leverage and makes shovels and spades easier to use than similar tools whose shafts simply round off at the end.

HEAD/BLADE: A thin, pressed-metal head is a poor bargain at any price. Some heavier stamped-metal heads are fine for light- to medium-duty work, but the best shovel heads are forged—hammered into shape rather than stamped out on machines. Forged metal is much stronger, longer-lasting, and less prone to bending out of shape; stainless steel is the finest choice. Tempering, a heat treatment, improves the quality of any metal. Some tools will display a gauge rating for the metal used to form their blades—typically 12 to 18. Higher numbers mean the metal is thinner, lighter, and more flexible; lower numbers mean heavier, stronger steel.

THE CONNECTION: The point where the head attaches to the shaft is where most shovels break under stress. To avoid this, select tools whose head connection extends farthest down the shaft—the longer the metal portion of the neck, the longer the tool will last. (Never use even the strongest shovel as a pry bar—it was not designed to remove boulders.)

BREAKING GROUND: Choose a shovel whose head is rounded or comes to a point. Use the footrests—not your arms—to push the head into the ground. When carrying a load of soil, always keep your hands close to the head of the tool and your body as close as possible to the shovel itself to protect your back and utilize your strength more efficiently. Never twist at the waist to turn and dispose of soil. Instead, move your feet and turn your entire body toward the area that will receive the load, *then* dump it. This will add only a few minutes to the task—but many years to your ability to perform it.

1. A nicely shaped shovel for breaking ground.

2. A poaching spade—as good today at transplanting perennials as it once was at unearthing the purloined beginnings of a fine rabbit stew.

3. A true handle makes shoveling or spading much easier.

4. Use a shovel with a flat or slightly rounded head when moving soil, compost, or similar materials; always keep the weight close to your body.

5. Put a foot up on one of those "rests" at the top of the blade and let your legs do the work, as George Balanchine noted Muhammad Ali did when boxing.

6. A well-made mini-shovel (real wood handle; steel blade) will become one of your favorite garden tools.

DOUBLE DIGGING: A tremendous physical workout that creates the perfect loose growing medium for raised beds. Divide the area to be double dug into foot-wide lanes. Remove the soil to a depth of one to two feet in the first lane, and place it on a tarp or in a wheelbarrow. Take a long-handled garden fork and jab it repeatedly into the bottom of the trench to loosen up the subsoil. Then shovel the dirt from the next lane into the first (if it does not all fit, add the extra to your pile), loosen up the soil at the bottom of that lane, and proceed until you have worked your way across the entire bed. When you are finished filling in the lanes, add any remaining soil to the top—this technique typically raises the surface of the bed at least several inches, despite all the rocks and large clumps of clay that have been removed along the way.

MOVING COMPOST, MANURE, AND SOIL: Use a shovel with a flat or slightly rounded head; these hold a larger quantity of material. Remember to keep your hands close to the head of the tool, the tool close to your body, and to never ever twist at the waist.

POACHING AND TRANSPLANT SPADES: These incredibly useful garden tools were originally designed to open up rabbit warrens quickly on private estates. Their long but compact heads make them the ideal tool for placing new plants in prepared soil and popping established ones out of the ground with a minimum of root disturbance (see below). Choose the length that best suits your needs.

POACHING SPADE TRANSPLANTING TECHNIQUE: To remove a small-to-medium size plant from the ground for overwintering indoors or for moving to a different spot during the growing season, slide a long-bladed spade straight down into the earth all around the perimeter of the plant, approximately six inches to a foot (depending on the size of the plant's crown) away from the stem or trunk. When this circle of cut soil is complete, slide the spade underneath the plant and simply pop it out of the ground with its roots tucked safely inside that island of soil. Plants can be moved about in this manner with no transplant shock whatsoever—*if* you perform the task in the evening (*never* in the morning or heat of the day) and water the plant immediately upon placement in its new home.

MINI-SHOVELS: These small, light shovels are perfect for making smallish holes or digging up medium-size annual plants; mine has become a "Top 3" favorite garden tool. Look for a solid steel head, a sturdy wooden shaft, and a secure D-shaped handle—not a pressed tin child's toy.

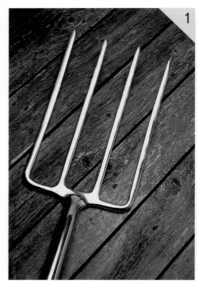

There are many helpful garden tools beyond the necessary basics of shovels, spades, and hoes. Here is a sampling . . .

GARDEN FORKS: Also called digging or spading forks, these are the heaviest-duty garden workers. When a shovel bounces off your rock-hard soil, reach for this relatively short-shafted, heavy metal tool with four or five flat "teeth." It will break up that soil wonderfully (most have no foot rests like those on a shovel or spade, but put your foot back there anyway for leverage). Flat-tined garden forks are also the tool of choice for prying up small-to-medium-size rocks (no boulders! Too big and even the tines on the best-quality fork will bend), and for plunging down repeatedly into the subsoil when double digging (see previous page). Some companies call similar tools with longer, thinner teeth garden forks as well, but they belong in our next category.

MANURE (OR COMPOST) FORKS: A cross between the true garden fork and the classic, hay-moving pitchfork (very long handle; three elongated tines), the "teeth" are longer and thinner than those of a digging fork, and there can be five or more of them. The more the better, as these are "turning" forks—their tines designed to be plunged into piles of compost or animal bedding to move or mix up the contents. They are also excellent for working loose soil, and—if the tines are close enough together—for picking up rocks and debris without bending over. The longer and thinner the tines of a fork, the more the tool should be used for turning materials rather than for breaking up unimproved soil.

HAND WEEDERS: These come in as many designs and variations as the full-size hoes whose task they share. The most basic is the classic, clawlike, handheld *cultivator.*

THE COBRA HEAD: A modern variation on the Yankee or New England style of weeder—the head of a swan-necked Warren hoe on a handle instead of on a long shaft. Very good at cultivating soil and making short rows, the Cobra also cuts off weeds well below the soil line, thanks to its head being sharp on all sides.

THE WEED HOUND (shown on page 16): Hand weeders require your getting down to the level of the weeds to dispatch them. Tools like the Weed Hound allow you to pop out dandelions and other deep-rooted weeds while standing up. No matter how you remove them, allow those weeds to dry in the sun and then chop them into your compost ingredients—the long roots are filled with minerals and essential trace elements pulled from deep in the soil, and composting will make those otherwise hard-to-find nutrients available to your garden plants.

PROPANE-POWERED FLAME WEEDERS: Perhaps the ultimate in no-work, stand-up weeding. They come in a variety of sizes—all the way up to backpack units fueled by refillable gas grill-size propane tanks! For most homes, a simple "yard and garden torch" style is sufficient. You screw a small, disposable camp stove-size propane bottle into the top of a long metal wand, click on the flame, and then wave the tip of the wand over the tops of annual weeds; the heat dehydrates them, bursting their cells and killing them without chemicals. Perennial weeds like dandelions will require a second pass a few days later—or a more lingering first encounter.

PRUNERS: A good pair of pruners is essential for cutting ripe bell peppers from their plants, thinning out overcrowded tomato vines, deadheading roses, and removing spent branches from large plants. There are two types—*anvil* and *bypass*. Like a hammer and anvil, the anvil pruner has one hard surface, which a single blade pushes against to cut; it is an easier tool to use than a bypass pruner (especially if you have limited grip strength), but it often crushes the branch rather than severing it cleanly. Bypass pruners act more like a pair of heavy-duty scissors; their cleaner cuts heal more rapidly—but they require more hand strength to use.

LOPPERS: You probably will not need a lopper in the average vegetable garden itself, but you will greatly improve the health of that garden when you use this essential landscaping tool to cut back encroaching brush and trees that are cheating your garden out of sunlight and airflow.

1. The sharp, flat tines of a true garden fork are unsurpassed for breaking up heavy soils.

2. A classic duo—the smallest shovel of all, the garden trowel, and the hand-held cultivator.

3. A manure, or compost, fork. The tines are longer and thinner than those of a heavy-duty digging fork, and more suited to moving loose material than earth.

4. The Cobra Head weeder. Sharp all around, the compact head slices through soil like a dolphin through water.

5. Propane-powered flame weeders dispatch unwanted plants with panache—and dehydrating heat.

6. Use the big loppers (top) to prune trees and shrubs that are cutting off sunlight and airflow to your precious plots. Make sure that small hand tools like these pruners (lower two) have brightly colored grips, the better to find them at the end of a long day.

7. Use pruners to trim excess greenery from overgrown tomatoes—and to pick your peppers; twist the fruit off by hand and the plant may never forgive you.

Water is essential to a productive garden—in more ways than you might expect. Yes, your plants need moisture to survive, and watering correctly can greatly enhance the health of your garden—but water is also the single most effective *pesticide* at your disposal.

WATERING WISELY: With very few exceptions, plants perform best when they receive an inch of water a week during the growing season—either from rain, you, or a combination. The best way to apply this water is in one long, slow session ("deep watering"). Never water your garden for brief periods every day; this encourages the development of shallow root systems—and the eventual rotting of those roots.

The best way to water when the time does come—after a week without rain—is to soak the garden overnight. If using a sprinkler or other overhead watering source, begin as late as possible in the evening (when plants are most receptive) and water until daybreak. Above all else, do *not* water overhead in the early evening, turn off the sprinklers, and let the garden sit wet overnight; this invites plant disease.

And, of course, keep all your garden soil covered with an inch of good mulch (see page 16) to keep that precious moisture *in* the soil. A well-mulched garden can easily go a week or more without water, while the same garden with bare soil may dry out within a day.

RAIN GAUGES: It takes quite a while to apply an inch of water. Place a rain gauge in the center of the garden and test your sprinkler; if it takes six hours to apply a full inch, turn it on at midnight and off at six a.m.—when the rising sun will quickly dry the plants. Inexpensive timers are available to turn the water on and off for you.

A rain gauge and notebook will help you keep track of Nature's contributions. Do not water simply because the surface of the soil seems dry. Instead, dig down 4 to 6 inches—to the root zone area of your plants. If it is dry down there, then yes—go ahead and water. (More likely, you will find the soil quite damp.) And never water only because your plants are wilting—especially if you have a heavy hand with the hose already; wilting is the prime symptom of an *over*watered plant. (Many plants will also wilt during intensely sunny days as a defense mechanism; these will look fine again by evening.)

In almost all cases, it is much easier to revive a plant that has gone too long without water than one whose roots are rotting from overwatering.

WATER WANDS: Many plants—roses, tomatoes, lilacs, etc.—dislike having their leaves wet. There is no way to avoid this during rains, of course, but it is easy to avoid when *you* are applying the water: Instead of overhead watering, use a water wand. These "rain heads on long tubes" allow you to reach past plant leaves and soak only the ground, not the foliage.

SOAKER HOSES: Available spiked with tiny pinholes or made of a material that "sweats" out drops of water. Lay them over bare ground around your plants and then cover them with mulch. All the moisture they produce will go right to the roots of the plants you wish to water—not onto their leaves or into your lanes to encourage weeds. Much more efficient and inexpensive to run than sprinklers, they use less water and waste almost none.

MISTING NOZZLES: Of course, spot watering is essential in some cases. Until germination occurs, a freshly seeded bed or row of lettuce, spinach, carrots, corn, beans, or peas should be soaked (sloooowly, to avoid washing the soil off the seeds) twice a day—first thing in the morning and last thing in the evening. A quality hose with a misting nozzle is perfect for this task. If rain is scarce, continue the morning watering for the first few weeks the young sprouts are up—but eliminate the evening spritz.

ADJUSTABLE NOZZLES FOR INSECT CONTROL: When aphids and other soft-bodied, smothering pests attack, simply brace the affected part of the plant with one hand and blast the creatures off with a sharp stream of water.

1. How *not* to water tomatoes. "Can" the watering can; it wets the leaves and invites disease.

2. Instead, use a water wand to get down where you can soak the soil, not the entire plant.

3. The "sweating" type of soaker hose. Such devices deliver a steady amount of water *very* slowly. Lay the hose down, cover with mulch, and you can water safely anytime—even during the hottest part of the day.

4. A misting nozzle delivers the perfect gentle spray of moisture for keeping a seedbed wet without dislodging the seeds.

5. Sprinklers can be very useful for watering large areas—especially during droughts. But do not run them for short periods of time; they are for long, deep watering only. Schedule the timing so that the sprinkler goes on late at night and stops just as the first rays of the sun should begin to strike your plants.

6. A high-quality hose will outlast and outperform a dozen discount duds. Do not scrimp on this garden essential.

7. The perfect pesticide. A sharp stream of water like this will kill 90 percent of the aphids it hits.

8. Multifunction nozzles like this offer a nice choice of settings, from a gentle mist for keeping seedbeds moist to a highly focused sharp spray that sends pests flying to their eternal reward.

software

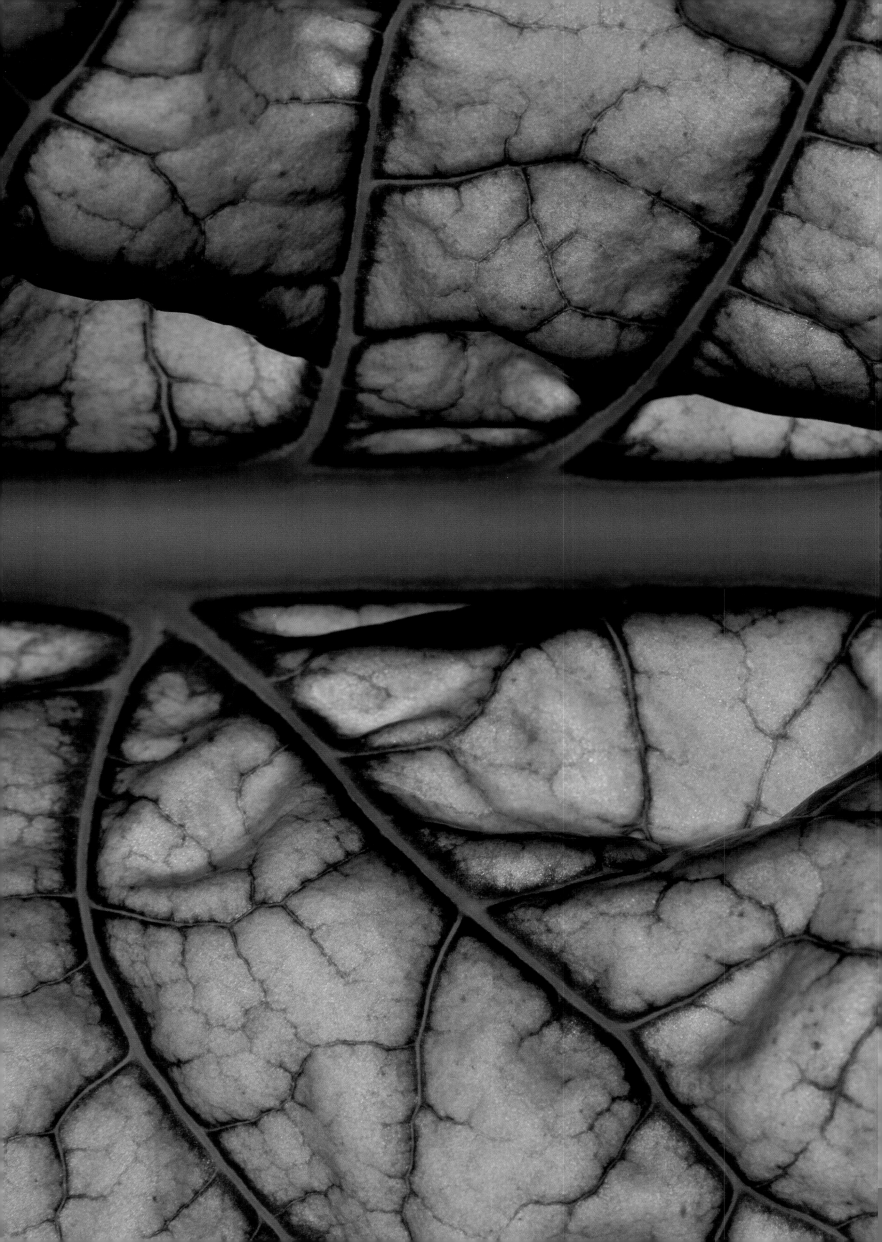

THE CYCLE OF LIFE

Starting your own plants from seed allows you to choose from a world of wonderful varieties unavailable to gardeners who simply buy their plants at garden centers.

CONTAINERS: Forget yogurt cups, egg cartons, and other household items—the results are rarely good. The size, shape, and construction of the six- (or four-) chambered containers nurseries use is ideal—that is why they use them.

THE SEED-STARTING MIX: Basically the same kind of light, loose, soil-free mixture recommended for containers—but without the compost. Seeds contain their own food and spring up better and healthier without any added fertilizer in the beginning. Mix up equal amounts of peat, perlite, and vermiculite, and add a tablespoon of lime or wood ash per five gallons of mix (see "Containers," pages 18–21, for more details), or use a premixed product like Premier's Pro-Mix. Do not use heavy bagged "potting soil"—*or* your equally heavy garden soil, which is likely also filled with weed seeds. (Could you tell which sprout is the pepper and which the purslane?)

TIMING: Start your sun-loving annual garden plants like tomatoes, peppers, and eggplant about six weeks before your "last average frost date" in the spring—for planting out at least two weeks after that date. Cool-weather lovers like broccoli and lettuce can be started a month earlier and placed outdoors while the nights are still quite chilly.

PLANTING: Fill your containers with mix and water them well—yes, *before* planting any seeds. When the mix is well saturated, place two or three seeds into each "cell," then cover them with a half inch to an inch of peat moss alone to prevent "damping off" disease, a fungal illness caused by overwatering. Peat contains natural antibiotics—it was used on old sailing ships to keep drinking water fresh—and allows you to keep your containers on the moist side without killing the plants within. Do not neglect this step.

GERMINATION: Mark your containers well (you can use plant markers or Popsicle sticks, but I prefer labels on the containers themselves—keyed to detailed descriptions in a notebook) and place them on a pie pan, cookie sheet, or other flat surface with a lip that will hold water. Then stretch clear plastic wrap overtop and place them where they will receive gentle bottom heat. Seeds need warm soil to germinate, and the best results are obtained when they sit on top of something that maintains a constant 70° to 75° temperature. An inexpensive electric seed starting mat is perfect for this. Otherwise, place your seeds on top of the refrigerator (where the warm air rises up from the compressor below) or on a flat-topped TV set. Do not cook them on a radiator or other overly warm area. And do not place them on a "sunny windowsill"; they do not need any light yet and it is likely to get very chilly there at night. Constant, gentle warmth is the key.

EMERGENCE: Check your setup every day to make sure the soil is still moist. If you do not see water droplets on the plastic wrap, give the soil a gentle misting—or bottom-water by pouring a little water into the tray for the drainage holes in the containers to take up. Do not pour water onto the tops of your containers—you will wash the seeds out of position and perhaps even out of their cells. Check daily for signs of sprouts and remove the plastic when the first one appears. The six-packs can remain where they are for another day or so to allow the remaining sprouts to emerge, but after that, they need to be moved into bright light.

ADOLESCENCE: A simple "shop light" containing a pair of four-foot-long Cool White 40-watt fluorescent tubes is ideal for growing sturdy young starts. Keep the tops of your young plants no farther than an inch away from the tubes; this is perfectly safe—fluorescent lights do not generate plant-burning heat. So-called sunny windowsills rarely work well—the developing plants need plenty of light to avoid that long, tall, "leggy" look, and most windows simply are not sunny enough, especially during the shortened days of the late-winter seed-starting season. Avoid expensive "plant lights" (most are too dim) and never use incandescent bulbs (too hot). After the first set of true leaves appears, give your plants a gentle feeding, replacing every other watering with compost tea or a dilute gentle organic liquid fertilizer.

1. Make your own seed-starting mix by combining equal amounts of peat, perlite, and vermiculite. Add a tablespoon of lime or wood ash per every five gallons of mix. The ingredients are dusty, so keep the mix moist.

2. Fill your seed-starting containers with the mix; old nursery "six-packs" work best.

3. Water your containers before planting; otherwise you may wash the seeds away.

4. Plant two or three seeds in each cell. Later, snip off the weakest sprouts with small scissors, leaving only the strongest, stockiest one behind for planting.

5. Butternut squash is an excellent choice for starting from seed indoors.

6. Gently squeeze the sides of your six-packs and the plants will pop right out, ready to plant.

7. This forest of basil sprouts is how the pros do it. Each cell is greatly overseeded; then, when the plants are a few inches high, they are "pricked out" individually with tweezers and transferred to individual pots.

8. Pepper starts in their six-packs await planting.

Cool season crops, like lettuce and broccoli, can go into the ground as soon as the plants have reached six weeks of age and the spring soil can be worked. For warm-weather lovers like peppers and eggplants, wait until the nights no longer dip below 50°. No matter what the crop, the plants should be at least six weeks old, and "hardened off" to prepare them for the harsher weather outdoors.

THINNING OUT: This is the hardest task for gardeners who start their own seeds. You *must* plant more than one seed in each cell to account for poor germination, but then most of your cells will contain multiple plants. Before planting, take a tiny pair of scissors and clip off all but the strongest plant in each cell. Do not keep the tallest plants; these light-starved, "leggy" specimens are often the weakest. A healthy start is short and stocky, with well-formed leaves and good color. You can attempt to transplant your extras to other pots if you wish; professionals deliberately do this—crowding their starts and then separating them out as they grow. But once plants begin to attain a good size, you *must* thin them out in some manner; leave more than one in each cell, and the results will be poor.

HARDENING OFF: When planting time arrives, take your plants outside for a few hours on a nice day, but bring them back in by nightfall. Repeat this a few times, gradually extending the time the plants spend outside each day until you finally leave them outdoors overnight. (Pay attention to the weather and be prepared to change plans if a sudden cold snap is predicted.) The transition from warm home or greenhouse to cold spring soil is a harsh one, and hardening off lessens that shock. Even store-bought starts will benefit greatly from this technique.

PLANTING: Choose a time in the late afternoon or early evening, after the sun has passed its peak but while there is still good light. Squeeze the sides of each cell in your six-packs gently until the plant pops out—do not try to pull it out by its leaves or stem. Dig a little hole with a trowel, toss in a handful of compost, place the plant on top of the compost, and fill in the hole with a mixture of compost and garden soil, bringing the plant's original six-pack soil level flush with the surrounding ground. Water well in a circle around the plant—not directly onto it— and then water a bit each morning until it rains. *Note:* Always plant in the evening. Never plant in the morning or during the day.

SPECIAL INSTRUCTIONS FOR TOMATOES: Unique among garden plants, tomatoes develop roots along any part of a buried stem (or even a branch). Two-thirds of your young tomato plant should wind up underground at planting time; if the plant is a foot tall, bury the bottom eight inches. Place the crushed-up shells of a dozen eggs in the planting hole to supply the extra calcium tomatoes require to taste their best and resist disfiguring blossom-end rot. Remove any leaves that are below the soil line, fill in the hole with a mix of compost and soil, and water well, avoiding the leaves.

DIRECT-SEEDING: With cool-weather crops that are traditionally direct-seeded, like lettuce, it is best to start the first runs indoors and transplant them outside, as the soil is generally too cold early in the season to sprout the seeds; then direct-sow the runs that follow. Crops like peas, beans, and corn simply do not transplant well, and direct-seeding is pretty much the only way to go. Prepare the planting bed a week in advance: Remove all weeds, smooth out the soil, water well, and wait for the weeds whose seeds you have awakened to sprout. Hoe these weeds out as gently as possible, dig a little trench, plant your seeds, and then cover the area with an inch or so of a seed-starting mix, compost, or screened topsoil. Moisten the ground well with a misting nozzle every morning and evening till the sprouts emerge—then stop all evening watering.

TIPS AND TRICKS: If you are a novice gardener unfamiliar with young plants, start a few seeds indoors of any crops you direct-seed outdoors, so you will know which sprouts are your desired crop and which are weeds. If the soil is on the cool side, soak the seeds of crops like peas in damp paper towels for one to three days before planting; just a day of such soaking will speed their germination greatly. After a few days, sprouts will begin to emerge from the seeds. Do not wait any longer than this—if the sprouts get too large, they will be damaged at planting time.

1. Cool-season crops like lettuce and broccoli can go into the ground as soon as the soil can be worked in spring. Lettuce is typically direct-seeded, but your first runs should be started indoors, as the soil will likely be too cold to germinate the seeds.

2. Squeeze the sides of your containers gently and the little plants should pop right out with their rootballs still nicely intact.

3. Always "harden off" new plants for a few days outdoors before planting them in the ground.

4. Be sure to position your plants at the same level in the ground as they were in their containers, except for . . .

5. . . . tomatoes, which should have three-quarters of their stems buried in the soil.

6. Although transplanting is *sometimes* achieved successfully by advanced gardeners using biodegradable pots made of peat or paper, peas much prefer being direct-seeded where they are to grow . . .

7. . . . as do beans. If the soil remains frustratingly cool at planting time, soak the seeds overnight in wet paper towels to hasten germination.

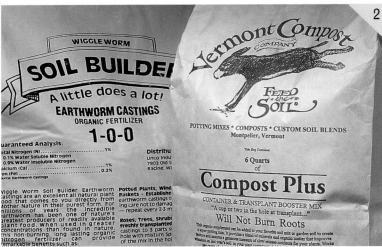

void packaged chemical fertilizers like Miracle-Gro; their concentrated salts build up in the soil, and the unnaturally fast, weak growth they produce attracts pests and disease. They are also unbalanced. A typical "10-10-10" or "30-30-30" chemical fertilizer may be *arithmetically* balanced, but plants do not use the three nutrients those numbers represent (see below) in equal amounts; most plants prefer a 3-1-2 ratio. (Because this *is* a ratio, fertilizers rated 6-2-4 are also ideal. Much higher numbers than 9–3–6 would be difficult to achieve using natural ingredients—and could be harmful to plants.)

NPK: All plants require three different basic nutrients: Nitrogen, Phosphorus, and Potassium. These are commonly represented by their respective symbols "N," "P," and "K" on packaged-fertilizer labels. A fertilizer with an NPK rating of 10-5-6 contains 10 percent nitrogen, 5 percent phosphorus, and 6 percent potassium.

NITROGEN: The single most essential food, "N" helps plants attain a good size and is especially important to nonflowering plants like corn (a notoriously nitrogen-hungry crop) and grass lawns. But nitrogen must be used with care on flowering plants; if they receive too much, they will grow big, lush leaves and not much else.

Barnyard manures are the classic natural source. Poultry manures (and packaged seabird guanos) are very nitrogen-rich (as high as 10 or 12 percent); use them to feed crops like corn and for mixing with "calmer" nutrients. Cow and horse manures are much gentler—and more balanced with other nutrients. Never use fresh manure in your garden; it should always be composted until it develops a sweet and earthy smell. And never use "manure" from meat-eating household pets like cats and dogs; it is not safe.

PHOSPHORUS: "P" is essential for strong root development and flowering. If plants are big but not blooming, stop all nitrogen feeding and scratch some phosphorus into the soil. One of the best natural sources is *bonemeal;* available bagged at virtually every garden center, its phosphorus content quickly becomes available to plants, making it the best choice for remedial application. Another excellent source, *rock phosphate,* is actually "heirloom bone meal"— the mined skeletal remains of prehistoric animals. Its considerable store of phosphorus is released gradually over time—making it a natural slow-release fertilizer. Rock phosphates are also rich in essential minerals and trace elements.

POTASSIUM: The all-around nutrient, "K" helps plants use other foods efficiently, improves their overall quality, and helps them withstand stresses such as climate and watering extremes. The best source is *greensand* ("glauconite"), a greenish, sandlike material mined from what were once ancient sea beds. Available bagged at garden centers, its label makes it appear to contain only a small amount of potassium. But that nutrient actually makes up 7 percent of this sand, which, like rock phosphate, releases its essential food to the soil slowly over time.

COMPOST: This humble fertilizer tops them all. It is simply perfect, containing all three major nutrients in their ideal proportions plus numerous minerals and essential trace elements that chemical fertilizers lack. More important, compost contains abundant soil life, which is necessary for plants to absorb *any* food—chemical or organic. Compost also raises the level of organic matter in your soil.

An inch a year is all most plants need to thrive. With most crops, it is preferable to mix the compost into the soil before planting. ("Don't feed your *plants*; feed your *soil*.") With disease-prone plants, however, apply that inch directly on the surface. If you feel your plants need a mid-summer boost, shovel another half inch around them, or give them a drink of compost tea.

COMPOST TEA: Fill a porous cloth container with compost and place it in an appropriate amount of cool water: a sockful in a gallon; a quarter of a standard-size pillowcase in a five-gallon bucket, or a full pillowcase in a clean trash can. After 24 hours, remove the "tea bag" and empty its contents back onto your compost pile. Pour the tea around the base of your plants or use it to give them a foliar feeding.

FOLIAR FEEDING: Most garden plants can absorb nutrients through their leaves if sprayed first thing in the morning (an hour or two after the sun rises), when their "pores" are open, drinking in the dew. Use a half-strength dilution of a gentle natural organic liquid fertilizer (such as a kelp/seaweed/fish mix) or compost tea (after straining it through cheesecloth to prevent clogging your sprayer). Use a clean, dedicated sprayer—*never* one that has held chemicals of any kind—and soak the plants well; whatever runs off their leaves will be used by the roots.

1. Barnyard "tea" bags. Drop one into a quart of water and pour the resulting brew for your thirsty plants.

2. If you cannot make your own, buy compost in a bag—or, even better, buy a bag of earthworm castings!

3. This glistening pile contains the unique blend of nutrients found only in earthworm castings.

4. A balanced, organic-based fertilizer and a natural growth hormone.

5. Guanos are gold! Bats do it. Birds do it. Peruvian birds apparently do it best.

6. Fertilizers made of seaweed, fish, and "marine cuisine" are tasty seafood for your plants. The last-named contains very hot nitrogen, thanks to its use of rich seafood shells.

1. Spun-polyester row covers protect plants from cold directly with their physical barrier and indirectly by trapping warm air underneath. The porous cloth allows air and water to enter—and a surprising amount of light.

2. A stretched-plastic greenhouse—the ultimate season extender. Freestanding greenhouses such as this always require their own heat source.

3. A classic cold frame filled with plants hardening off in the spring. The glass cover on the right will be placed atop the entire frame at night to keep out cold air.

4. Elegantly classic glass cloches protect young pepper plants from frost. Other plant protectors may be more practical, but none are half as ornamental.

5. Inexpensive plastic cloches like these also do the job—and they stack for easy storage.

Many gardeners struggle with frustratingly short growing seasons, often *just* lacking enough time for long-season crops like habanero peppers and full-size watermelons to ripen fully outdoors. And all gardeners must contend with unpredictable weather—hard frosts that strike weeks after a region's "last average frost date" in the spring (nothing defines the *true* meaning of "average" in that phrase better than a field full of frozen plants) and early fall cold snaps that always seem to precede frustratingly long and pleasant Indian summers. And so we fight back—with devices that offer protection against unseasonable snaps, the ability to extend the season those few weeks in either direction—and, sometimes, much more.

ROW COVERS: These rolls of light, diaphanous, spun-polyester fabric are often simply called Reemay, after the best-known brand name. Stretched over arching metal hoops, they allow air, water, and a surprising amount of light through their fabric—but keep frost and insect pests outside. Row covers allow in so much light that crops requiring no insect pollinators, such as carrots and cut-and-come-again stands of salad greens, are often protected by them all season long—the plants enjoying the slightly warmer temperatures and almost total protection from insect pests the covers provide.

Row covers offer gardeners the opportunity to put out cool-weather crops like spinach and broccoli weeks earlier in the season; the covers prevent the damaging physical effects of frost *and* maintain a soil temperature many degrees warmer than the outside air. At the end of the season they perform the same function again, protecting late runs of fresh greens long after frost would otherwise finish them off. They can also be raised up off the ground and utilized as shade cloth in midsummer, to cool off plants threatened by a too hot and sunny stretch.

Even gardeners who do not challenge the weather treasure Reemay for its ability to protect plants against insect pests—even fruiting plants like squash and eggplant. The covers provide a physical barrier against pests like squash bugs and flea beetles early in the season, when the smallish plants are most vulnerable. By the time the covers must be removed to allow pollination (when the plants' flowers open), the pests have often moved on in frustration. And even if they have not, the larger plants can now tolerate their attentions much better.

COLD FRAMES: The classic cold frame has been protecting plants for as long as there has been glass to cover it with. Cold frames can be made of anything from boards, stones, or hay bales topped with an old windowpane to intricate devices with automatic temperature-controlled venting systems. What they all have in common is a place for plants—either in containers or in the ground—surrounded by some type of insulating protective frame, with a moveable clear panel on top.

Cold frames can make excellent substitutes for plant lights early in the season. The young plants can be taken out of the house as soon as they are a few inches tall, and transferred to the protection of the cold frame instead of the glow of fluorescents. Keep the glass cover on at night and during cold, cloudy days. On sunny days, however, the inside can quickly become a hothouse and must be vented to prevent overheating. Automatic vents that work via a gas-filled cartridge lift that lid just the right amount without human intervention—or electricity—and drop it back down when temperatures plunge. The old-fashioned way to achieve this is with a stick—jammed under the glass sideways to allow just a crack of an opening on a cold but sunny day, and propped up straight to open the frame wide on a gloriously warm one.

Angled toward the south, cold frames provide young transplants with all the sun they need while hardening them off at the same time. In the fall, they can be planted with a late run of greens that—with any luck—will still be available for harvest many days into the winter.

FRENCH HOT BED: Cold frames can also be used to create a French hot bed—an ancient technique in which the bottom of the frame is layered with several inches of steaming fresh horse manure, then several inches of soil, then plants or seeds. The heat generated by the manure warms the inside of the frame as efficiently as if it were the inside of a greenhouse, while the crops grow in clean soil, well above the source of that heat. A properly made hot bed will germinate lettuce seeds in January in the North.

CLOCHES: These are just as ancient as French hot beds. Technically meaning any item used to temporarily cover a single plant early or late in the season, the name most often brings to mind classically beautiful bell-shaped glass plant protectors. Perhaps more practical are the plastic variety; unbreakable and stackable, they offer excellent—if not as elegant—frost protection. *Note:* Like cold frames, cloches concentrate heat on a sunny day no matter how cool the air temperature, and are best used overnight only.

GREENHOUSES: The ultimate in season extension. Their stretched plastic or glass tops keep out frost and capture all the light young plants require, but they can be expensive to heat. Those attached to the side of a house are much more energy-efficient; freestanding greenhouses require their own heat source.

Kitchen gardens provide the freshest possible food, close to its place of preparation. The gardeners who tend them cook to the seasons, with meals and menus following suit as cool-weather crops give way to the fruits of summer, the bounty of fall, and end with a reprise of spring, as the final harvests mirror the first.

As winter retreats, fall-planted garlic begins to sprout. Lettuces go into the ground, quickly surrounded by broccoli, beets, and radishes. When the soil warms a bit, spinach is seeded, along with a second run of salad greens.

A few garlic sprouts are harvested with scissors—not too many or you will reduce the size of the bulbs—for a little taste of the indispensable herb to come. The perennial herbs begin to green up; now is the time to clip off the old, browned parts—and perhaps harvest a bit of fresh new growth.

Fall-planted pansies, happy to have made it through the shortest days, resume their growth—their first flowers will be colorful and delicious.

Get the peas in the ground before April 1 or vine-killing heat will arrive before their tasty pods! Watch the vines carefully, and begin to pick as soon as the first ones are ready (carefully—do not hurt the plant! Hold the stem with one hand as you pull off those sweet little pods with the other). The more peas you pick, the more pods the plants will produce.

Now the heads of broccoli are ready. Slice them off with a sharp knife while the buds are still tightly closed, cutting at an angle so rain runs off the stem and the plants survive to produce delicious mini-head "side shoots" in the fall. If cauliflower leaves are shy about covering their white heads, provide a bit of help with clothespins and string; do not delay, the season moves quickly now, and too much sun will ruin that perfect pale color.

Time to plant new herbs and perhaps an early tomato. Have row covers and cloches close at hand, pay attention to forecasts—and keep most of your warm-weather plants inside a bit longer for insurance. As herbs grow quickly, harvest daily with scissors; no life has too much spice. Deliberately neglect a few closest to the center of the garden—the beneficial insects and pollinators who come for the nectar and pollen their tiny flowers provide are the best friends your homegrown pantry could have.

Now the soil seems warm and the race begins. Out come the main-crop tomatoes, peppers, eggplants, cucumbers, and squash. Push your finger down into that soil. It *is* warm! In go the seeds of string beans, dried beans, and corn. When *those* plants break ground, summer is here.

Watch the garlic like a hawk. Cut off and savor the scapes as soon as they appear atop those artistically curling necks. When the bottom leaves turn brown, harvest your "stinking rose" crop and spread it out in a cool spot. Sort out any cloves that have burst their skins and use them immediately to create a garlic-flavored feast.

Schools close down for the season, pea vines begin to brown, and the last of the early radishes and beets are eaten. A second run of string beans is planted where the garlic once grew; a late run of corn replaces lettuce that can no longer take the sun.

Spinach is harvested in finalé fashion, not cut-and-come-again style *this* time, but uprooted—the pumpkins and watermelons can wait for this bed no longer!

The first green tomatoes yield to red—bring them in just before they finish so the sun cannot steal their fabulous flavor. Green peppers grow large—leave them alone! The color and taste to come will be far superior.

Sweet corn silks and tassels: If the patch is small, give it a hand and move pollen into silks—every grain that lands in a silken hair becomes a candy-sweet kernel on a cob. When the ears are big and full and the silks begin to brown, peel back a husk and pierce a kernel; if white liquid squirts out, boil the water and warm the butter—you will soon taste summer.

Now the race is *truly* on: Pick the fresh beans daily or the plants will stop producing. Harvest ripe tomatoes before heat and light can lessen their taste. Clip your kitchen herbs before they can flower and become bitter.

Sweet "green" peppers finally reveal their beautiful true hues—and the sugars and nutrition that have so slowly developed within; *now* you can pick them wisely.

Then you need a bigger harvest basket. Then more than one basket. Then more than one basket several times a day . . .

And then, all too suddenly, the days grow shorter. The dried beans are ready—do not delay; frost would ruin your season-long investment!

The tomato plants begin to turn brown. But this is no time for tears. Broccoli rewards being left in place by sprouting new heads again. Plants past their prime go to the compost pile, replaced by spinach and lettuce seeds that sprout so much faster now than in spring—the soil holding its warmth even as the air so quickly gives it up at dusk.

Then school bells fill the air and it is time to plant garlic and pansies once again. The circle is complete. The final runs of lettuce and spinach go to sleep under their ghostly white row covers just as a hard frost redesigns the garden.

And you dream of spring.

Rosemary

Most members of the thistle family are weedy pests—but not the globe artichoke. A true Mediterranean delicacy, the plants behave as short-lived perennials where the ground does not freeze in winter. But in most of the United States, they must be grown as annuals, started fresh every spring.

SCIENTIFIC NAME: *Cynara scolymus*

TYPES: Green and purple. The green varieties include Green Globe (grown in the Mediterranean climate of central California, this is the type most often found in markets) and Imperial Star, which produces a nice head from spring-started seed in a single season in the North. The purples—mostly heirloom Italian varieties like Violetta—are hardy, and certainly more ornamental, but lose their royal hue and turn green if cooked for more than just a minute or two.

GROWING TIPS: The ideal locale has cool spring and summer weather but no hard freezes— the central coast of California is perfect. In the North, start the seeds very early indoors and transplant out to the garden when all threat of frost is gone but the weather is still cool; finicky young artichokes despise frost yet require several weeks of temperatures below 50° to set those edible buds.

HARVEST: Cut the developing flower heads off the plant an inch below the base when they are well formed and tight. Do not let the flower begin to open or you will have grown nettles! In mild climes, the plant will continue to produce for several years.

BUYING: Look for small, tight heads (the smaller the head, the more edible parts inside—even the stem is tasty in tiny ones); reject any whose flower buds are beginning to open.

STORAGE: Tight, fresh heads will keep in the refrigerator for a week or two. Freeze the whole flower head in heavy plastic for later use, or pickle the flower hearts.

TRICKS: Cool spring weather is essential; if Nature might not cooperate, refrigerate the started plants for two weeks. Make sure developing plants stay well watered, especially in warmer climes.

1. Unique in flavor, the inner leaves will always prove to be the tastiest part of the plant.

2. Some varieties have a pretty purple blush to their leaves—mimicking their thistle cousins.

3. A classic head. Look for leaves that cling tightly like this; reject ones that are already opening up.

This wondrous seasoning comes in an unmatched multitude of flavors and shapes. One could fill a large garden with basil plants, each a unique version of this versatile herb, and still leave a good half of the available varieties ungrown.

SCIENTIFIC NAME: *Ocimum basilicum*

TYPES: The Genovese varieties—the traditional Italian basils—are prized for pesto making. Specialty types include holy basil (*Ocimum sanctum*), revered in India as a culinary herb and traditional Ayurvedic medication, and the many flavored (lemon, lime, cinnamon etc.) varieties. The purple types are ornamental, vigorous, productive, and add a unique hue to pestos and tomato sauces. Unlike most purple plants, basil keeps its color when cooked.

GROWING TIPS: Basil is extremely frost sensitive and tries to flower very quickly—often just weeks after transplanting. Begin harvesting leaves as soon as they are of size, or keep pinching off the growing tips to prevent bud formation (the flavor of most herbs tends to change for the worse when flowers appear). This pinching also produces bushier plants.

HARVEST: Use scissors, early and often! Heavily harvested plants produce abundant leaves.

BUYING: Look for full-grown plants, with their roots still attached, in tall, ventilated plastic bags; this new style of packaging keeps the herb fresh a long time in the refrigerator. (Try harvesting some of the leaves and then planting the roots.)

STORAGE: Picked leaves should be used promptly or frozen. Do not dry them—they lose their flavor. If fresh basil is overly abundant, make and freeze pesto. You can pull up entire plants (especially when frost is threatening), roots and all, shake off excess dirt, and store them upright in an inch of water in a plastic bag in the refrigerator without loss of quality for weeks.

TRICKS: Many ornamental basils can more than hold their own in the flower garden, especially the miniature, shrublike Spicy Bush and fancy-leafed Purple Ruffles. Allow some plants to produce their tall spikes of white, red, or purple flowers; although the leaves will not taste quite as good, they will still be perfectly edible—and those beautiful blossoms will attract beneficial insects to the garden (see page 14), making the flowering herbs an ideal companion plant to crops suffering insect insult.

1. Purple-leafed basils, seen here forming a dramatic backdrop in a community garden, are ornamental and should be planted in highly visible areas.

2. Unusual and highly ornamental, this column-shaped Australian basil develops a woody stalk as it ages.

3. Harvest frequently with scissors or pinch the growing tips—and don't be shy—if plants go unpicked or unpinched they will quickly produce flowers, with the leaves losing flavor as a result.

4. Many gardeners plant extra basil so that they can enjoy the pretty flowers—and use their pollen and nectar to lure beneficial pest-eating insects to the area.

Opposite page: Delicious and ornamental Thai basil.

Most garden picking is done early in the morning, but string beans—also known as snap or (even if yellow or purple) green beans—must wait till later; their leaves will take revenge if handled while wet with dew.

SCIENTIFIC NAME: *Phaseolus vulgaris* ("regular" bush and pole beans)

TYPES: *Bush bean* varieties have been bred to stay close to the ground and do not require any support; the gourmet favorites French, filet, *haricots verts*, etc., fall into this class. *Pole beans* require something to grow on and include many unique ornamental varieties—especially in their extended family—such as "yard-long" or asparagus beans (members of the *Vigna* species) and the beautiful runner types (*Phaseolus coccineus*), like Scarlet Runner—which span both our categories, as they can be eaten young as green beans, or dried.

GROWING TIPS: In dry climes, crowd bush types together; in damp ones, give the plants some breathing room. Grow pole beans on the sturdiest trellis (or bean tower) possible; mature vines will topple a weak support. Adding a natural bacterial inoculant (available in seed catalogs and larger garden centers) to the soil allows the plants to convert nitrogen in the air into food.

HARVEST: Harvest often, using scissors to prevent damage to the rest of the plant. Pick just when the pods are beginning to swell—the plants stop producing if pods develop full-blown mature seeds. Filet and other gourmet beans must be picked especially young; they get tough and stringy at full size.

BUYING: Look for uniform color, small size, and crispness; large beans with overly visible pods will be tough even with their "strings" removed.

STORAGE: Refrigerate in a plastic bag if the beans were harvested when the air was cool. If harvested in the heat of the day, use them all that evening.

TRICKS: Bush beans tend to mature faster than pole beans; plant a small run every two or three weeks for a continuous harvest.

1. It may take the vines of pole bean varieties a month or so to become established and reveal their true exploratory natures—especially if planted early in the season. Resist the temptation to sow the seeds too thickly. Because . . .

2. . . . mature vines will stretch 15 feet or more, and require a sturdy trellis with plenty of surface area for them to use on their "climb" back down after reaching the top. Make the trellis strong but not overly tall; if you cannot reach the top to harvest the beans before their seeds reach full size, the plants will slow down—perhaps even stop producing.

3. The yard-long or asparagus bean has the climbing habit of its relatives, the true pole beans. The elongated pods make a great garden attraction and taste delicious.

4. The flowers that precede bean pods are among the loveliest in the world of edibles.

Opposite page: These perfectly picked beans have just the right bit of bulge for the best taste.

The best dried beans are homegrown. They cook more quickly and have a much finer taste than store-bought—and are much less likely to cause the best-known side effect of bean eating. Beans for drying are available in an almost inexhaustible number of (often legendary) heirloom varieties—like Cranberry, Midnight Black Turtle Soup, Maine Yellow Eye, and Ireland Creek Annie. The Seed Savers Exchange has records of over 4,000 different varieties.

SCIENTIFIC NAME: *Phaseolus vulgaris*
TYPES: Most "drying" beans are *bush* types that require no support and tend to produce all their fruits at once. But some varieties are *pole* (climbing) beans, while others are *half runner* types—either really tall bush beans or really short pole beans. Their name comes from the fact that they are often left to sprawl ("run") on the ground—which is never a good idea.
GROWING TIPS: The opposite of beans for fresh eating: Check regularly for pests, but otherwise leave unharvested until the pods are almost brittle. Never touch the plants when the leaves are wet. Never crowd plants that are growing beans for drying, and be sure to provide good airflow around the patch.
HARVEST: When the beans and the weather are dry. Do not water their area of the garden for at least a week before you plan to harvest. If it rains, wait until a few days after it stops to pick.
BUYING: Only buy dried beans that have been kept in a cool, dry environment. Freshly grown dried beans purchased at a farmers market in the fall will be vastly superior to store-bought.
STORAGE: Make sure beans are completely dry before storage, then seal tight in jars and keep in a cool, dry place. If you notice little holes in any of your beans (from bean weevils), freeze the entire dried crop for 24 hours before long-term storage.
TRICKS: Grow one of the many varieties that can also be harvested when the seeds are still green and used like limas (these are often called "shelling beans") or one of the few varieties, like Buttergreen and Scarlet Runner, that can be eaten pod and all (like string beans) when young. Harvest some fresh, and leave the majority on the vine for drying.

1. Provide sturdy support for the types that do choose to climb; these Scarlet Runner vines may reach 20 feet in length if the season is warm and long.

2. The beautiful flowers of the Scarlet Runner bean attract iridescent hummingbirds with their bright red color. The beans that will follow can be eaten young and fresh as string beans, when plump as limas, or . . .

3. . . . can be left alone and allowed to dry into the most colorful seeds that exist in all of horticulture.

Opposite page: A riot in beantown.

Beets are an ultimate crop—every part of the plant is edible, and you cannot possibly harvest them too early. In Northern climes, grow them all season long; where the weather is mild, all *year*.

SCIENTIFIC NAME: *Beta vulgaris*

TYPES: The round red ones we know so well (*globe* types) are an "improvement"; in the eighteenth century, all beets were either cylindrical or pointy at the bottom end (called tops after the ancient spinning toy). The cylindrical varieties generally have the tastiest roots. All three types come in many colors, including white, purple, "Golden," and the popular Chioggia, an heirloom with red skin and candy-cane insides.

GROWING TIPS: Sow the "seeds" (actually little fruits containing several true seeds each) directly in the garden in spring, after the hard frosts are over; light chills will not bother the plants. Clip off (and eat) all but one of the multiple sprouts from each seed, then thin (and eat) those until the remaining plants are a good three inches apart. You can harvest some early greens without compromising the final beet, or grow some just for their nutritious spinach/chardlike greens: Big Top and Tall Top produce large amounts; and the heirloom Lutz Green Leaf (also known as Winter Keeper) produces great leaves—and a root that can stay in the ground the longest without getting woody.

HARVEST: Early and often. You can enjoy this often dazzlingly ornamental edible from sprout to full-size—but do not leave any variety other than "Lutz" in the ground too long or the roots will get tough.

BUYING: Reject any with overly hairy roots. If the option exists, choose the ones with the freshest-looking greens—and enjoy those too!

STORAGE: Keep greens in the fridge, washed, patted dry, and placed in a plastic bag or standing in a tall container with a few inches of water in the bottom. For short-term root storage, wash, dry, and keep in a cool, dry place. For storage over winter, harvest right *after* frost (which sweetens the roots), remove the tops, wash and dry the roots, and store in moist sand below 40°.

TRICKS: Plant varieties with amazing greens, like the burgundy-colored Bull's Blood, in the flower garden. To preserve the color of the roots, bake them or leave a few inches of the tops and all of the skin on while boiling.

1. Grow your own candy canes! The heirloom variety Chiogga does not look like much from the outside, but a slice through the center reveals concentric circles of color.

2. The color of a golden beet is not just beautiful; such vibrant drama reveals that the flesh contains more important nutrients than drabber-hued foods.

3. The top growth of some varieties can be strikingly attractive; plant these types where the leaves can catch the light of the sun shining through their veins.

4. Most beets are grown in the kitchen garden for their tasty and nourishing roots—but the above-ground growth is also delicious in recipes that call for cooked greens.

Perhaps the single healthiest food we can eat, blueberries are enormously rich in disease-fighting phytochemicals and Number 1 in natural antioxidant (cancer-preventing) content—more than broccoli! Easy to grow in a home garden, a couple of blueberry bushes would look great nestled among azaleas—whose need for highly acidic soil they share.

SCIENTIFIC NAME: *Vaccinium* species

TYPES: The highbush varieties (*Vaccinium corymbosum*) produce big, tasty berries on plants that grow up to 6 feet tall and make a fine "edible fence" when planted close together. Gardeners down South should grow Southern highbush or rabbiteye (*Vaccinium ashei*) types, which do not need as long a winter chill. Low-bush (*Vaccinium angustifolium*) types, popular in the Far North and Canada, are groundcover plants that grow only a foot or so tall; the berries are small, but extremely tasty. All types have showy and long-lasting scarlet fall foliage.

GROWING TIPS: Blueberry bushes absolutely require an acidic (pH 4 to 5.5) soil; fill at least half of their planting holes back up with peat moss. Like azaleas, they are thirsty and have delicate roots, so mulch heavily and stay a step back when harvesting. Bushes are self-fertile, but you will get larger, better-tasting berries if you plant multiple varieties.

HARVEST: Ripe fruits are always fully colored and come off easily in the hand; if a berry resists a gentle tug, let it ripen a bit more.

BUYING: Berries in vented plastic containers travel and store better than ones in paperboard, which tend to get moldy. Inspect all packages carefully for signs of mold or damaged berries, and reject any whose bottoms show stains.

STORAGE: Sort through carefully and remove any that are bruised, battered, or moldy; put the rest in a vented plastic container; they will keep in the fridge for weeks. Blueberries freeze better than any other fruit. Do not wash them first—just freeze in solid plastic quart and pint containers, then rinse before use.

TRICKS: Plant one bush each of an early (Duke), early-mid (Patriot), mid (Bluecrop), late (Jersey), and very late (Elliot) season variety to have the longest possible fresh harvest season.

1. Highbush blueberry plants produce the biggest fruits—most at a very comfortable picking height.

2. Watch for the flowers to appear, followed by green fruits. Do not pick berries until they are *fully* colored up, when taste and nutrition have reached their peak.

3. Birds—otherwise very beneficial visitors to the kitchen garden (see page 14)—love blueberries. Netting applied over the plants can be helpful, but it is much better to hang such protection on supports, so that berries can ripen safely beyond the range of little beaks.

4. The perfect dessert, blueberries taste best without adornment. Try some frozen on a hot summer day.

The florets we so enjoy are actually clusters of unopened flowers. One of the few true vegetables, broccoli is probably the most health-enhancing of all the nonfruit edibles—from tiny sprouts (especially rich in natural cancer-fighting phytochemicals) to full-grown heads.

SCIENTIFIC NAME: *Brassica oleracea* (mostly in the *Cymosa* group)

TYPES: "Grocery store heads" are modern hybrids. Older, open-pollinated Italian varieties produce smaller, multiple heads over a longer period of time. The heads of sprouting broccoli are smaller and more numerous still. The buds and leaves of broccoli raab (*Brassica rapa,* botanically closer to turnips) are popular as cooked greens, especially in Italian sandwiches. Broccoflower, cauli-broc, Romanesco (almost triangular cauliflower-like heads), and similar curiosities are crosses between broccoli and cauliflower; in the garden, the shape of the leaves reveals the strongest lineage.

GROWING TIPS: These classic cool-temperature crops bolt in hot weather. Young plants should go in the ground as soon as spring frosts are over. Fall crops do better in many locales.

HARVEST: Always before flower buds begin to open. Main crop varieties: Cut the stalk on an angle (so rainwater runs off) when the heads are big, hard, and tight, using a sharp knife. Take smaller heads anytime they seem full and tightly packed. Clip sprouting and raab types cut-and-come-again style whenever you want.

BUYING: Choose hard, tightly packed heads of uniform color with very firm stalks.

STORAGE: Wrap the heads in plastic and place in your refrigerator's crisper. For longer storage, cut, keeping a nice length of stalk, and place in a container with a few inches of water in the fridge. Broccoli freezes very well; blanch it briefly first. Or puree florets (alone or with seasonings) and freeze in heavy plastic pints or quarts.

TRICKS: Always leave plants in the ground after cutting the main head in spring; most will produce numerous "side shoots" (tasty miniature heads) for the rest of the season. In mild climates, fall-harvested plants may even produce a flush the following spring. If a head's flowers begin to open, leave it; the yellow blooms are numerous and colorful and attract pollinators and other beneficial insects to the garden.

1. Broccoli seeds will not germinate in too-cool soil, but the cold-hardy young plants can be started indoors and then go into the ground very early in the season.

2. When these flowers begin to appear, the heads are past their prime. When this occurs . . .

3. . . . check the rest of the crop, and harvest those heads whose florets have not yet begun to bud. Leave the ones that *have* begun to flower alone if you have the room; their pretty yellow blooms are abundant—and lure helpful insects into your garden to pollinate summer crops and devour troublesome pests.

Opposite page: A weirdly shaped and wonderfully colored cross between broccoli and cauliflower, Romanesco's lime-green flower buds have a decidedly pyramidal bent.

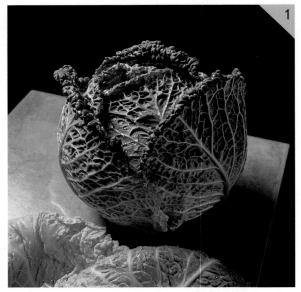

This big, showy member of the cancer-fighting brassica family rivals root crops in its ability to store well for long periods of time without refrigeration, keeping many families nourished over the winter in the days before electricity became common. The plants are rich in vitamin C, and most types can be stored from Thanksgiving till spring—even longer when turned into coleslaw or fermented into that German specialty, sauerkraut.

SCIENTIFIC NAME: *Brassica oleracea capitata*
TYPES: *Ball* is the kind you are most likely to see in stores and home gardens; smooth-leafed, round, smallish two- to four-pounders in either the standard green or beautiful red (burgundy) color; good for storage, fresh eating, and kraut making. The crinkly, curly blue-green leaves of the *savoy* types are so attractive that the plants are sometimes used in strictly ornamental gardens; mild-flavored and of medium-size, they are better for fresh eating than long keeping. *Flat tops* have truly flat heads and are the preferred choice for serious sauerkraut makers. The classic heirloom variety Early Jersey Wakefield typifies the *pointy-head* types; considered the absolute best-tasting cabbages, they must be harvested promptly in late spring to prevent splitting.
GROWING TIPS: Cabbage likes a very rich soil, high in organic matter. Set plants out right after the last spring frost to give this cool-weather lover enough time to mature before the weather turns hot. Or direct-seed in summer for harvest after the first light frosts, which will sweeten the flavor.
HARVEST: When the head is nice and tight, cut it off with a sharp knife, leaving an inch of stalk behind (spring-sown crops will regrow a smaller head for fall harvest).
STORAGE: This is where cabbage shines! Forget the fridge: Remove the loose outer leaves, wrap the heads in newspaper, and store singly in a cool, dark, and moist area; they will keep for many months at 40° or below. Or dig a hole in the ground, line it with straw, place the heads in upside-down, then cover with 4 to 5 inches of shredded leaves and dig them up one at a time when you are ready to use them.
TRICKS: Use red cabbage to make colorful and tasty coleslaws and krauts.

1. The distinctively crinkly leaves of a savoy variety.

2. Early Jersey Wakefield. Many feel this heirloom variety is the best tasting of the cabbages.

3. A Napa cabbage. Use this beauty in Chinese cooking.

Opposite page: Red-colored cabbages have it all over the greens—pests do not seem as attracted to them, home gardeners find them easier to grow, they are obviously more ornamental, and their color reveals superior nutritional value.

Carrots are one of the things you have never really tasted unless you have grown your own. Most store-bought carrots were harvested quite a while before you had a chance to buy them—and they still taste pretty good. But a carrot pulled fresh from the ground is candy sweet, rich with a flavor that will not be nearly as intense even a few days later.

SCIENTIFIC NAME: *Daucus carota sativa*

TYPES: A wonderful diversity: Miniature versions like Thumbelina; the classic, blunt-tipped Nantes varieties (considered the sweetest); long, pointy-tipped Imperator types (the ones most commonly found in supermarkets), and more. Purple carrots are *not* a new development—they are throwbacks to the old originals from which modern orange carrots were selectively bred centuries ago.

GROWING TIPS: Carrots do *not* like a lot to eat. Strong fertilizers—even natural ones—make them hairy and woody. Because you do not want to walk on their nice loose soil, carrots are ideal for raised beds and containers. The seeds are excruciatingly tiny (20,000 to the ounce); mix with dry sand and broadcast—then thin so that each carrot has several inches all around to grow. (A BB-like coating makes pelleted seeds easy to sow individually.) Keep the planting bed moist till sprouts emerge, then mulch to prevent weeds—carrots' worst enemy.

HARVEST: If your soil is nice and loose, just grab them by the shoulders and gently pull up the roots without breaking them. If it is heavy, dig up the whole plot from the outskirts and sort through it on a carrot search.

BUYING: Look for smooth, uncracked roots; reject "hairy" bunches; they were overfed and will not be very sweet. If available, choose blunt-tipped varieties over pointy ones.

STORAGE: Always remove the green tops promptly, and wash before storage. Put them in vented plastic bags in the coldest part of your fridge, or try the classic: Layer the roots in wooden boxes filled with sawdust or sand in a cool, dark place; they will keep nicely till spring.

TRICKS: Carrots are biennials, only setting seed their second year. Leave a few roots unharvested and the next spring their tops will produce a huge flush of tiny white flowers in an umbrella-like shape (like Queen Anne's lace); these umbelliferous blooms will lure beneficial insects like aphid-eating ladybugs and lacewings to your garden.

1. Carrot greens reveal tasty roots below. If the roots are unharvested, the biennial plants will produce tiny white flowers atop these greens the following year.

2. Promptly removing the green tops of carrots keeps them crisp in storage. Although thin, these carrots are close to two feet long—a sign that they were grown in perfect soil.

3. The long, pointy tips identify these Imperator-style carrots. Blunt-tipped types are generally sweeter.

Opposite page: When carrots are grown in heavy clay soil, the roots will often separate out, or "fork"—frequently creating amusing shapes at harvest time.

This wonderful plant is so close a cousin to broccoli that there is often disagreement over which category a specific "heading brassica" belongs in. (Generally, the plant's leaves will hold the answer.) One thing is certain—if the head is white in color (or *should* be), it is a cauliflower. Gardeners, however, will fare better with purple varieties, which tend to be less fussy (and *highly* ornamental).

SCIENTIFIC NAME: *Brassica oleracea botrytis*
TYPES: White-headed types are the classics, and are best planted early in the spring. The lime-green types include the mixed marriages like broccoflower, cauli-broc, brocoverde, and perhaps Romanesco (see page 60); these are best grown for fall harvest. The purples have cauliflower-like leaves and plant growth but a decidedly broccoli-like taste, and most of the heads look like broccoli. (If you want to keep the purple color, enjoy these heads raw.)
GROWING TIPS: A cool-weather-loving crop, cauliflower also requires a very sweet (alkaline) soil; in areas with acidic soil, dust the earth with lime or wood ash before planting. To remain white, heads must be protected from the sun after they form. The more colorful varieties do not require blanching, and some (especially the purples) will produce edible side shoots after the main head is cut.
HARVEST: When the heads are hard and dense; better too soon than too late. Do not nick white heads—they will turn black quickly.
BUYING: Look for tight *white* heads; brown, yellow, or black spots are signs of over-ripeness, age, or harvest injury. Choose a dramatically colored variety if available.
STORAGE: Store homegrown heads with the cut stem in water in the coldest part of the refrigerator. Use store-bought heads promptly. Whiz up some in a blender and freeze for a winter soup.
TRICKS: The classic way of blanching white varieties is to tie the biggest leaves over the developing head. Or choose a self-blanching variety like Andes, whose leaves grow up as opposed to out, curling naturally over the head and theoretically protecting it without your help (at least you have bigger leaves to work with). *Note:* Self-blanchers are very heat-sensitive and should be grown only in the coolest weather.

1. A purple cauliflower. The head looks more like broccoli, but the leaves reveal the plant's true heritage.

2. The classic white cauliflower. Unlike broccoli, whose heads are formed of many flower buds that will open if not harvested promptly, the tight "curds" of cauliflower are composed of aborted buds that will not bloom. When they age, they simply pull away from each other.

3. A lime-green "mixed marriage." The curds scream "cauliflower," but there is broccoli in those genes.

Growing this member of the carrot family is a challenge even for the best backyard grower. It requires moisture and fertilizer in amounts that would kill or ruin almost any other crop. It also needs constant warmth—it is the only crop that bolts if it gets even a little *cool*. (If the temperature drops below 55° several days in a row, celery may simply go to seed.) Try growing celeriac (aka celery root) instead—this unusual plant, with its celery-growing-out-of-a-cue-ball look, still needs a lion's share of water and food, but not celery's warmth—although it does demand a growing season at least four months long.

SCIENTIFIC NAME: *Apium graveolens dulce* (celeriac is *Apium graveolens rapaceum*)

TYPES: You will be lucky to find one celery in most catalogues, but there *are* several types: the traditional green one; one with a red blush on some stalks (Giant red stalk); another (Red stalk) that stays red even when cooked; and Golden self-blanching, which may allow you to achieve those almost white centers of the commercial varieties if, despite the name, you hill up the plants to keep sunlight away from the interiors.

GROWING TIPS: Keep the plants wet and well fed and do not allow the air temperature to drop below 55° for three or four straight months, and you've got it made . . . if the weather does not get too terribly hot.

HARVEST: Before it flowers (generally 80 to 100 days after planting), when the stalks are about 18 to 24 inches tall.

BUYING: Check the top edges—if they seem severely cut (actually recut) or are overly brown, it may have been sitting too long. Really fresh celery will still have its top leaves.

STORAGE: Set the entire plant into a few inches of water at near-freezing temperature (40° is almost too warm).

TRICKS: Although it looks more like parsley, a plant also in the *Apium* genus (subspecies *secalinum*) called "cutting celery" (aka leaf celery, soup celery, smallage . . .) has the taste of celery but is much easier to grow.

1. These familiar green outer stalks . . .

2. . . . create a living fence that blanches the inner parts by shielding them from the sun.

3. Look for clean, undamaged specimens like these in the store. More greens would be better.

4. Celery seeds and herbal extracts that contain their essence are natural anti-inflammatories.

Opposite page: Celeriac produces a huge root with celerylike stalks on top; the taste is all celery and the plant is less fussy to grow—and quite the garden conversation piece.

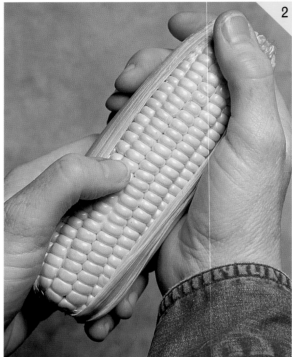

It is no accident that one of the finest varieties of this giant edible grass is named Ambrosia. An ear of sweet corn picked at the peak of its ripe, sugary perfection, cooked for the briefest of moments, slathered with butter and consumed with sartorial abandon, is total joy.

SCIENTIFIC NAME: *Zea mays*

TYPES: "Normal sugary" ('su'): All the old open-pollinated varieties and many hybrids, including the almost eponymous Silver Queen. "Sugary enhanced" ('se' or 'se+') corns have been bred to be sweeter and to hold that sweetness for a longer time after picking. Never plant su or se types near a "super sweet" or "shrunken" variety ('sh' or 'sh2'), bred to be *ridiculously* sweet and to hold that sweetness even longer after picking. Mixing their incompatible pollens will cause all your corn to taste awful.

GROWING TIPS: Provide plenty of water, a rich soil, and supplemental food (corn is a notoriously heavy feeder). Six "plant blocks" (6 rows of 6 stalks each—36 plants) is a minimum size for getting nice full ears.

HARVEST: Note the date when half the plants have silk visible; the ears should be ripe three weeks later. Peel back a husk and pierce the third row of kernels with your fingernail; if the liquid inside is white and milky, the corn is ready.

BUYING: Coolness is *everything!* Even "fresh from the field" farm-stand corn that was picked that morning will taste bad after being warm all day. Choose ears that are cool to the touch and that feel full all the way to the tip. If you can strip them, pick the ears whose kernels are in the straightest lines; crooked rows indicate uneven watering or incomplete pollination, both of which limit potential sweetness.

STORAGE: Don't! Bring water to a boil, turn off the heat, quickly pick and shuck the corn, plop it in the water for less than two minutes and eat. When you buy corn, take a cooler and refrigerate on the spot. At home, keep ears unshucked in the fridge and use promptly. Or, blanch the shucked ears for just an instant, cut the kernels off the cob, and freeze immediately.

TRICKS: Hand-pollinate small plantings by rubbing the pollen off the tassels and down into the silks; every pollen grain that lands in a silk becomes a kernel. Bite into a fresh-picked ear right in the garden to experience its ultimate sweetness.

1. A good-sized stand of corn; the more plants you grow, the bigger the ears and the more rows of kernels per ear. If you have the room, use it for extra plants.

2. Look for ears whose kernels are in nice straight lines. Those ears will be the sweetest.

3. White corn? Yellow corn? Split the difference and buy or grow one of these bicolor varieties.

4. Some colorful corns typically grown for drying and grinding taste as sweet as Silver Queen if picked at the "milk stage."

Corns grown for drying should stay on the stalk until their husks turn brittle—so they can provide us with popcorn and the makings of distinctive breads, muffins, chips, and more.

SCIENTIFIC NAME: *Zea mays*

TYPES: Popcorn: A huge diversity of cob sizes and kernel colors—which, alas, always pop up white. Dry field corns, aka Indian corn, are grown for grinding into flour. Flint corn kernels stay big and full looking when dry. Dent corn kernels shrink and thus have "dents" in them. "Flour" or "starch" corns grind into a *very* fine flour. The color range for all types is enormous: vibrant reds, rich blues, jet blacks, bright pinks—even metallic green, silver, gold, and fabulous mixes emerge as the kernels dry. Single-colored flour corns (especially red and blue) keep their color through the final product; mixed colors tend to grind up white with specks.

GROWING TIPS: The more plants, food, sun, and water the better. Stop supplemental watering after the silks have browned.

HARVEST: During a dry spell. If a long rainy time is predicted, get the crop inside and allow it to finish drying in a cool, dry place. Never harvest when wet.

BUYING: Flour corns: Try a farmers market, where you can make sure the "ornamental corn" has not been shellacked. It is much easier to find fresh popping corn on the cob. In both cases, dryness is key; reject any ears that seem the least bit flexible.

STORAGE: After harvest, hang in a cool, dry, well-ventilated area. When you are ready to use it, hold the ear firmly and twist; the kernels should come off in your hand. If they do not, they are not dry enough. Store kernels with moisture-absorbing (silica) packets in tightly lidded glass jars. Double-grind flour varieties only as needed —not all at once. Like the highest-quality coffee beans, the vibrant flavor of fresh-ground cornmeal will astound you.

TRICKS: Some varieties, including Bloody Butcher, Mandan Red, Aztec Black, Anasazi, and Rainbow Inca, are dual purpose—sweet corn when young, drying corn when old. Harvest some ears for fresh eating and leave the rest to dry on the plant.

1. Pull back the husks to help your corn dry completely. Leave them in place for decorative effect.

2. The color range of drying corn is enormous.

3. Double duty! Display your ornamental corn in a dry place for Halloween and Thanksgiving and then pop the kernels to decorate your Christmas tree.

Light, airy, crunchy, and refreshing. And pickles! Through simple curing, cucumbers have gone beyond being a clever way to preserve the harvest to become a true staple on their own.

SCIENTIFIC NAME: *Cucumis sativus.*

TYPES: The basic distinction is between pickling and fresh-eating (slicing) types—although many cuke fanciers say they prefer the taste of pickling types for fresh eating, and all cukes will pickle very well. There are seedless cukes and "burpless" ones (these very thin-skinned varieties are easier to digest, but rarely available in stores), as well as Armenian (*Cucumis melo,* technically a melon) and Asian varieties.

GROWING TIPS: Grow them on a trellis or fence—this lessens the chance of disease and yields 20 percent more fruit, which will be longer, straighter, tastier, and easier to find. Make sure they get plenty of calcium (crushed eggshells or bonemeal) to keep them crunchy.

HARVEST: You cannot pick cukes too early; the smallest ones are the tastiest. Do not let them get bigger than the seed package recommends or they will be mushy and the plant will stop producing. (You may need to harvest daily at the peak of the season.)

BUYING: Check for firmness; a limp cuke will likely have an off-taste. Reject any with yellow spots (unless you are lucky enough to find a naturally lemon-colored variety like Boothby's Blonde or lemon); a green one showing signs of yellow was left on the vine too long.

STORAGE: Most cucumbers will stay fresh for a couple of days left out in a cool spot (50° to 60°) in the house. Do not refrigerate. If you do, these tropical fruits will be in sad shape when you try to use them later; they are best eaten right away, or made quickly (before they lose moisture and crispness) into pickles.

TRICKS: You do not have to heat up the house to make "refrigerator pickles": Combine a cup of water, a half cup of vinegar, a tablespoon of brown sugar or honey, and a little salt, heat until almost boiling, then pour into a clean, quart-size glass jar filled with freshly cut slices, chunks, or spears and a little herbal seasoning (garlic, dill etc.); put the lid on and place in the fridge once cool. These will taste just like true "put up" pickles and keep for weeks!

1. Presumptuous labeling. Perhaps these freshly picked farmers market beauties *will* be processed into pickles, but so far they are still simply cucumbers.

2. Bush varieties are a good choice for small gardens; they produce a lot of fruit on a compact plant rather than on the classic sprawling vine.

3. Treat them right and every flower will become a thirst-quenching fruit. Be sure to pick those fruits on the small side for the finest taste and longest harvest.

How appropriate to follow cucumbers with dill—whose flavorful leaves and seeds are essential for pickling! One of the oldest herbal remedies known, dill seeds have long been used as a cure for indigestion, flatulence, colic, insomnia ("dill" may be derived from a Norse word for lulling someone to sleep), and are a fine source of dietary calcium. But dill leaves taste best when picked *before* the plant flowers—so grow twice as many plants; some for leaves, some for seeds.

SCIENTIFIC NAME: *Anethum graveolens*

TYPES: Technically, there is a biennial (flowers its second year) and an annual version, although only the annual is cultivated. Fernleaf (or featherleaf) varieties are the frilliest, and could easily claim a "ferny" spot in the ornamental garden. Varieties with Dukat in their names tend to be sweeter; and Superdukat claims the highest essential oil content, which means a more intense flavor and better medicinal results. Bouquet has large leaves, and Mammoth has them on a *big* (up to 4-foot-tall) plant.

GROWING TIPS: Much better to plant the seeds directly in the garden; seedlings are often fussy about being transplanted.

HARVEST: For the tastiest and most aromatic leaves, harvest often to prevent the plant from setting seed; pick individual leaves or cut back the top third of the plant. For the wonderfully aromatic seeds, harvest leaves lightly (if at all) to allow prompt flowering; those flowers will be replaced by seedpods; when *their* color starts to change, harvest the entire head and extract the seeds when dry.

BUYING: Aroma is all; *smell* that little bundle—if the fragrance is pungent, the dill is fresh.

STORAGE: Freeze or dry the leaves. Hang the spent flower heads upside down over white paper and shake well to collect the seeds. Or, "store" both in pickled form as you preserve the rest of your harvest.

TRICKS: To insure a good supply of *leaves,* plant a fresh run of seeds every three or four weeks throughout the season. Position plants intended for *seed* harvesting near "buggy" garden trouble spots —dill flowers are some of the best at attracting pest-eating beneficial insects.

1. The attractive, fernlike foliage of dill contains one of the most powerful and distinctive of all the herbal flavors.

2. Seedpods appear after the flowers fade; allow these to dry on the plant as long as possible, and harvest during a dry spell to obtain . . .

3. . . . the seeds that are so essential to pickling and other culinary uses.

Opposite page: Dill flowers are very attractive—both to our eyes and to insects whose main diet is garden pests. The clusters of tiny blooms arranged in an umbrella-like shape are a powerful lure for the best "beneficials."

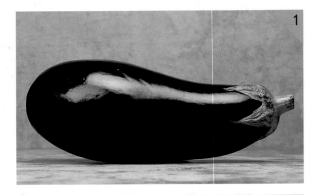

A bit tricky to grow, but well worth the effort. Eggplant is perhaps the most "meaty" of all the garden edibles, adding a deep flavor and texture to vegetarian dishes. All the flowers and many of the fruits are also highly colorful and ornamental, making the plant appropriate in otherwise nonvegetable settings.

SCIENTIFIC NAME: *Solanum melongena*

TYPES: There are many colorful and showy varieties available in addition to the large blackish-purple traditional Italian types (of which Black Beauty is the classic variety). Fruits can also be long and slender or small and round, and come in delicate light greens, neon pinks (Neon), purple/lavender with white streaks (the classic Rosa Bianca, considered by many to be the best-tasting), and even pure white (Snowy, which is long, and Easter Egg, which is small and round).

GROWING TIPS: Eggplant requires warm weather, and it should be one of the last plants to go into the ground in spring. For the best-looking fruits, stake the plants like tomatoes (this is essential for keeping long, thin varieties from touching the ground).

HARVEST: Promptly! If left on the plant too long, eggplant becomes bitter. Cut plants free with scissors while the skin is still glossy (classic types) or before the color changes (ornamental and unusual varieties). Do not worry about harvesting too soon—eggplant is one of the best vegetables to eat at the "baby" stage, and frequent harvesting will keep the plants producing new fruits.

BUYING: Look for good color in the ornamental varieties (white should be *white,* not yellow; neon pinks and purples should be bright) and good skin gloss in the classic types.

STORAGE: Like tomatoes, eggplant should not be refrigerated; store at cool room temperatures (55° to 70°) and use quickly. Slices may be peeled and dried for long-term storage, and miniature and long, thin varieties can be pickled whole. Freezing works best when slices are breaded and partially or completely cooked first.

TRICKS: Protect young plants from destructive flea beetles with floating row covers (see page 40) early in the season; this will also keep the tender plants a bit warmer and speed their growth. Remove the row covers when your plants' flowers open for pollination.

1. The traditional "black" Italian type; perfect for oriental stir-frying and breaded slices.

2. The color range of the more ornamental varieties is astonishing; place showstoppers like this right up front in your flower garden.

3. Beautiful, orchidlike eggplant flowers are the most elegant produced by any of the edible plants.

Cousins to radicchio and chicory, the two distinctly different plants we call endive—"AHN-deeve"(true endive) and "EN-dive" (Belgian endive)—are essential components in soups and salads. Both are somewhat similar to lettuce, but with very different leaf textures and a generally sharper flavor. Neither, however, should ever have a bitter "bite"—and will not if you grow your own.

SCIENTIFIC NAME: *Cichorium* species

TYPES: Scarole, escarole, and similar spellings are simply types of broad leaf endive *(Cichorium endive);* the frilliest (highly ornamental) types are often called *frisée* ("free-ZAY," French for curly). Belgian endive is not an endive. This well-known (and more French than Belgian) edible is actually the sprout of a true chicory *(Cichorium intybus)* root, always grown in complete darkness to prevent a bitter taste.

GROWING TIPS: For the tastiest leaves, grow true endive (Belgian is grown indoors) in fall rather than spring. If the weather drops below 50° for a few days in spring, the young plants will bolt while still small and be useless. Sow seeds directly where you want the plants to grow in late summer, and harvest young for best taste. Endive will simply not grow from mid-spring through late summer.

HARVEST: Best when clipped frequently, cut-and-come-again style, with scissors. If larger plants are desired, blanch the centers by using clothespins to hold the outer leaves tightly closed over the developing heads. Blanched or not, inner leaves have the best flavor.

BUYING: True endive: Look for small heads; the centers should be a much lighter color than the outer leaves—otherwise, it will all likely taste bitter. If possible, sample a bit of an inner leaf—this will tell the tale. Belgian: Smaller is still better; look for tightly wrapped leaves with no traces of brown.

TRICKS: To force your own Belgian endive, grow a true chicory (such as Witloof) in the garden, dig up the big root at the end of summer, pot it up in a very sandy mix, put it in a cool (barely above freezing), dark place for a month, then bring it into a warm area (like under the kitchen sink), water well, put a bag over it to exclude all light, and begin harvesting tasty yellow or red shoots ("chicons") in about two weeks.

1. Frisée is an especially frilly type of true endive; the centers are blanched to produce the tastiest leaves.

2. Belgian endive is neither Belgian nor endive. This popular salad ingredient is instead the top growth of a chicory plant whose full-grown root has been harvested and then forced to produce these familiar shoots indoors in darkness. The standard yellowish/white types are produced by the classic Witloof variety.

3. Endive's first cousin, radicchio.

4. True endive is a lettucelike plant grown outdoors; it is the escarole in classic Italian wedding soup.

Opposite page: A colorful reddish-purple tone distinguishes the Treviso type of Belgian endive—a red-leafed variant of the classic Witloof.

Fennel's aroma is unmistakable, as is the feathery foliage that adorns one of the tallest herbs you can grow (up to 8 feet). Savor the anise-flavored leaves and seeds of some types, the celerylike "bulb" of others. This somewhat tender perennial (certain to overwinter safely only in zones 7 and higher) belongs in the flower garden, where its vibrant, sometimes colorful foliage stands out and its beautiful yellow flowers are right at home.

SCIENTIFIC NAME: *Foeniculum vulgare*

TYPES: Bulbing (Florence; Finocchio; sweet fennel) varieties are smaller (2 feet high), and are grown for their above-ground, rootlike bulbs, which have a distinctive anise flavor, rather than for their leaves. The seeds are generally found in the vegetable sections of catalogues. Leaf fennels are grown for leaves and seeds, and include varieties that are green, bronze, and bicolor; they can grow very tall and are considered herbs.

GROWING TIPS: Bulbing types grow best in fall; keep well watered and clip off stems to prevent flowering. Leaf: Look for slow-bolting types and harvest cut-and-come-again style to prevent flowering (unless you mostly want the seeds). Leaf types will always bolt (go to seed) their second year.

HARVEST: Pick bulb types when the base begins to thicken. Harvest the growth of leaf types anytime (unless the seeds are quickly desired—then leave the plants alone).

BUYING: Look for medium-size bulbs; reject any overly thick ones. Look for fresh, colorful leaves —and, of course, a strong anise scent.

STORAGE: Bulbs keep well in a cool, dry spot or in the fridge. The delicate leaves should be used promptly or recut and refrigerated standing in water in a tall plastic or glass container.

TRICKS: Chew the seeds or brew them as a tea to soothe indigestion. Substitute fennel for dill seeds as a kitchen change of pace. If a caterpillar feeds on the plant, let it be if you can—it will become a large, beautiful swallowtail butterfly. The umbelliferous flowers attract the most and best beneficial insects to your garden.

1. The feathery foliage of fennel produces one of the herb garden's most intense and welcome scents.

2. The multiple small flowers of dill are just the right size to attract beneficial insects. Although the main diet of these helpful little bugs *is* garden pests, they also enjoy the pollen and nectar these flowers contain.

3. If seeds are your culinary goal, avoid harvesting the leaves and allow those flowers to form. They will be followed by seedpods like these, rich with treasures to be released when they are dry.

Opposite page: "Finocchio," or bulbing fennel.

There is no need to choose between a garden of edibles and a garden filled with flowers; grow plants whose blossoms are a treat to eat *and* to behold. More than just a pretty face, many flowers do delicious double duty—whether grown in an ornamental or a kitchen garden. From the surprising spiciness of nasturtiums to the capillary-curing potential of the rutin-rich blossoms of pansies, violets, and violas, you can have your flowers and eat them too!

TYPES: Nasturtiums *(Tropaeolum majus)* have a climbing habit; both the leaves and flowers deliver a distinctive spicy-tangy flavor; the Jewel varieties are considered the best-tasting. Pansies *(Viola* species) are cool-weather lovers that continue to produce their nutritious blossoms long after cold-weather crops have gone to sleep. Marigolds *(Tagetes* species) have an unearned reputation for repelling pests, but their flowers provide welcome color in the vegetable garden—and some varieties (mostly in the Gem series—*Targetes tenuifolia)* make a welcome addition to fresh summer salads. The petals of the most popular edible variety, Lemon Gem, can be used in place of saffron to flavor and color rice. Other flowers with edible blooms include some of the calendulas, agastaches, garden pinks *(Dianthus deltoids),* salvias, hollyhocks *(Alcea ficifolia),* monarda (bee balm), borage—and, of course, rose petals.

GROWING TIPS: Nasturtiums (climbing) and edible marigolds (erect) are annuals grown in summer; mix a few in with your vegetable plants—the flowers will attract extra pollinators to the area, resulting in more flowers and more traditional edibles. Common garden pansies can take the coldest of climes but burn up in hot weather; plant them in the fall ("overwintering pansies") for harvest through the following spring. Grow violets, Johnny jump-ups, violas, etc., in the spring—or, even better, harvest wild plants, which are richer in rutin than cultivated varieties. Never eat rose petals or flowers from unknown sources—they may have been sprayed!

1. "Daisy" and "chrysanthemum" can mean many things—the scientific names and categories for the many plants with those common names have shifted greatly over the years. This restaurant-quality specimen was offered for sale as "Daisy: *Gandesblume chrysanteme."* Do not consume "daisies" or chrysanthemums unless you know them to be an edible variety.

2 and 3. Pansies, violas, Johnny jump-ups—all the *Viola* species produce blooms that are not only edible, but are also the best natural food source of rutin—a hard-to-find but essential nutrient with the power to strengthen capillaries and thus lessen the disfiguring effects of spider and varicose veins.

4. and 5. Both the leaves and flowers of nasturtiums are delicious—and, unique among the edible flowers, their flavor provides a hot bite much like that of a mustard leaf.

Opposite page: Beautiful borage flowers. Though borage is best known for the edible oil produced from its seeds, its leaves and flowers are also tasty salad additions.

HARVEST: Pick nasturtiums (flowers and leaves) throughout the summer. Pick pansy family flowers frequently and use to accent salads. Pick off edible marigold heads and place on salads whole or quartered. Use fragrant rose petals sparingly as a salad accent.

BUYING: Edible flowers are being offered for sale at more and more retail locations. Be careful *only* to buy flowers clearly marked as "edible," no matter how safe you know the basic variety (for example, pansies) to be. *Never* eat flowers from a florist's shop or similar venue—they may have been soaked in pesticides!

STORAGE: Pick the blooms early in the morning, store loosely packed in lidded plastic or glass containers in the refrigerator, and use promptly. Or, pick in the evening after the sun has gone down for immediate use. Never pick during the heat of the day; the flowers will wilt before you can get them inside.

TRICKS: You can "store" whole flowers in a living arrangement; cut with a few inches of stem attached and then float your harvest "face up" in a marble-filled bowl of clean, cool water right out on the table.

WARNING: *Not all flowers are edible!* The badly misnamed garden "sweet pea" *(Lathyrus odoratus*—not a member of the *Pisum* edible pea family), for instance, is an extremely poisonous plant; as are foxgloves, calla lilies, and many others. Do not sample flowers unless a number of reliable references assure you that they are indeed edible. And avoid all flowers grown in gardens that are subjected to toxic sprays and other chemical controls.

1. Eat a dragon with your mixed greens! These snapdragons (*Antirrhinum majus*) create dramatic—and delicious—contrast when perched atop a mix of bronze, red, and green lettuces.

2. *Dianthus* flowers (garden pinks, cottage pinks . . .) are pretty to look at, both in the ground and in the salad bowl.

3. Lemon Gem marigolds; old garden books would have you believe these flowers keep slugs, rabbits, and other garden pests at bay. The truth is that both slugs and bunnies love them—they are edible, after all. Research *has* found that marigolds will deter some microscopic pests like the Southern root knot nematode, but only when the flowering plants are tilled into the soil before planting a crop the nematodes typically attack.

4. These edible orchids were grown in the glasshouses of Holland and shipped to America for restaurant and individual gourmet salad adornment. Their fresh look is surprisingly long-lasting when the blooms are protected in a closed plastic container and chilled. The taste is surprisingly juicy and chewy.

Opposite page: Pair edible marigolds with multicolored lettuces for a superb salad combination of colors, flavors, and nutrients.

Easy to grow, beautiful in form and color, peerless in flavor. Plant individual cloves in the fall. Come spring, they will awake, their leaves will grow tall, and—on most types—a serpentine stalk will appear, capped by a pod ("scape") that is wonderfully tasty when clipped young and sautéed in olive oil. Then, just as spring turns into summer, pull up the plants to discover a whole bulb for every clove you planted.

SCIENTIFIC NAME: *Allium sativum*

TYPES: Softneck (includes the white supermarket garlics; these store the longest without sprouting) and hardneck or stiffneck types (aka topset garlic; easier to peel, these types come in a riot of colors and sizes—including many wonderful heirlooms—all of which send up that central stalk mid-spring). So-called elephant garlic is actually a big leek (*Allium ampeloprasum)* that looks like garlic on steroids and has a mild, somewhat garlic-like flavor.

GROWING TIPS: In general, hardnecks perform better in cold climates, soft necks in warmer ones (like California). In very cold climes, mulch the planting bed with shredded leaves after the ground has frozen for the winter.

HARVEST: Begin checking your plants for doneness when the bottom leaves have turned brown; if a sample bulb is nice and plump, harvest it all. Do not delay, or the paper wrappers will split and the crop will be ruined. Do not wash.

BUYING: Search out locally grown garlics at farmers markets in season. In the supermarket, reject garlic kept in a chilled section.

STORAGE: Never refrigerate garlic! After harvest, cure for a few weeks in a warm, dry place. Do not remove the stems. Braid softnecks by those stems and hang in a cool, airy spot. Tie (unbraidable) hardnecks together loosely and hang. Use damaged bulbs first, and save the largest cloves for replanting.

TRICKS: Clip some shoots in early spring and use these garlic-flavored greens as you would cloves, but take only one cutting or you will reduce the size of the bulbs. To make your own intensely flavored garlic powder, peel, slice, and completely dry some cloves, grind into a powder, store in a closed jar, and use *sparingly*.

1. Plant large individual cloves in the fall. Depending on the weather, the cloves may sprout that year; it matters not. Mulch the ground well with shredded leaves after the soil has frozen hard for the first time.

2. In spring, the green shoots will grow quickly. As the season progresses, hardneck types will send up these beautiful serpentine stalks from their centers. Little bulges ("scapes") will soon appear atop those curling necks. Harvest them as soon as they appear, cutting them off the stalk with scissors just below the bulge—do not remove the entire stalk or the garlic may rot.

3. Harvest the entire crop when the bottom leaves turn brown. Hang the plants to cure for a few weeks before long-term storage.

Weird, wonderful and doubly misnamed, this plant has nothing to do with Jerusalem or artichokes. "Jerusalem" is a misheard corruption of either *girasole* (Italian for sunflowers) or Terneuzen (a city in Holland famed for its true artichokes). The "artichoke" part? Apparently someone once thought there was a resemblance between the plants. There is not. Nevertheless, this perennial does deliver a double dose of garden fun—an edible tuber underground and (in most varieties) masses of chocolate-scented yellow sunflowerlike blooms up top. (That is why it is sometimes called "sunchoke" or "perennial sunflower.")

SCIENTIFIC NAME: *Helianthus tuberosus*
TYPES: Only one, itself a member (along with true sunflowers) of the daisy family. A few varieties of this American native are available; always choose one that produces flowers.
GROWING TIPS: Needs no help from you. In fact, this plant is highly invasive. Grow it inside strong, deep edging or other containment—or dig up *all* the tubers at the end of the growing season; otherwise, you may have nothing but Jerusalem artichokes in your garden.
HARVEST: The pretty blooms for cut flowers anytime; the root at the end of the growing season, preferably after frost has killed the aboveground growth. Eat the tubers raw, cooked like potatoes, or dry and ground into flour.
BUYING: Look for heavy, well-defined tubers and avoid dried, shriveled-up specimens.
STORAGE: Freeze whole tubers or store in plastic bags in your refrigerator's crisper.
TRICKS: When freshly harvested, the tuber's carbohydrates are in the form of inulin, a non-sucrose sugarlike starch that some consider an ideal food for diabetics. (Others maintain it is simply not digested in this form, and has no food value.) In storage, this inulin slowly becomes a typical starch, making the tubers much like potatoes. (Native Americans fermented the roots, causing this change to be to sugars instead of starch.) Position your crop so that the exceptionally tall, full, fast-growing plants screen off unwanted views in summer. Jerusalem artichokes are a "mixed garden" all by themselves: Wait till the end of the season to harvest the tubers, but cut the flowers and bring them indoors all summer long. The more you cut, the more the plant will produce.

1. Jerusalem artichoke plants produce edible tubers underground; when fresh, their sugar/starch content is considered ideal for diabetics.

2. Surprise! Most of the plants that produce those tubers bloom beautifully aboveground as well. A member of the daisy family, many of the blooms this plant produces have a wonderful chocolate scent. Check catalogue descriptions carefully to make sure your planting tubers will produce these lovely flowers; a few types only provide the underground harvest.

1

2

3

A member of the huge and healthful brassica family, kale is essentially a type of cabbage that does not form a head and so looks more like lettuce, but with the taste of cabbage (and vastly superior nutrition—including a host of naturally occurring cancer-fighting compounds). Most varieties are striking in form and color—some familiar types are so attractive (and frost-proof) they are sold strictly for ornamental use in winter flower gardens. But ornamental only means they are pretty—all kales are edible.

SCIENTIFIC NAME: *Brassica oleracea acephala*

TYPES: Flat-leafed, curly-leafed (looks quite a bit like parsley), "crimpled" (some varieties look like miniature palm trees), ornamental, and really odd ones like the "walking stick cabbage" (aka Jersey kale or Jersey cabbage)—a 6-foot high "tree cabbage" whose tall, straight stem makes a striking garden conversation piece. Collard greens are in the same family as kale—and although we associate those greens with Southern climes, they taste better harvested in cool weather. Red kale is actually a different type of brassica *(Napus pabularia).*

GROWING TIPS: Sow seed directly where you want the plants to grow; many varieties do not tolerate transplanting. Probably the most frost-proof edible, kale loves growing pretty much anytime the weather is not really hot. Crops sown in fall can—and should—be harvested throughout the winter. (As with most cold-weather-lovers, frost improves the flavor.)

HARVEST: Anytime. The baby leaves are especially tasty when harvested cut-and-come-again style for use in mixed salads. Harvest larger leaves the same way. Cool weather harvests have the best flavor and color.

BUYING: Small leaves are better than big; reject any with brown edges or limp leaves.

STORAGE: In plastic bags in the crisper section of your fridge.

TRICKS: Some varieties (such as Redbor) start out green, but turn red when cool weather arrives; plant these in a visible area in late summer and watch the show!

1. Green-leaf kale—all colors of this crop are bursting with cancer-fighting nutrients.

2. A blue-green variety.

3. The color range of these plants is enormous. Small, thin leaves like these have the best flavor.

Opposite page: A red-leaf variety. These pretty kales look right at home nestled among hostas and other foliage plants in an ornamental setting. The shade in such leafy gardens also helps the leaves of the cool-weather plants stay sweeter when summer's heat arrives.

The edible from another world. This strange member of the brassica family looks more like a little spaceship than part of a nutritious meal— the result of a stem that "bulbs out" instead of growing up. Some say it has the crisp flavor of an apple, others describe it as nutty, and some call the taste a cross between that of turnip and cabbage. Eat it cooked, eat it raw, or just let it sit out and confuse your friends.

SCIENTIFIC NAME: *Brassica oleracea gongylodes.*
TYPES: Red-fleshed, which tends more toward the purplish, and white-fleshed, which is generally more of a delicately light lime-green.
GROWING TIPS: Sowing seed directly generally yields better results than transplanting. Although a cabbage family member, kohlrabi can handle heat better than most of its cousins. Grown throughout the season in the North, it is still a spring- or fall-only crop in the South. A naturally rich soil facilitates the fast growth necessary for the best flavor.
HARVEST: Greens, anytime. The aboveground, rootlike stems (corms) are best when young and small—no bigger than a tennis ball. The smaller the bulb, the better for raw eating.
STORAGE: In the crisper section of your fridge.
BUYING: Look for small specimens (observe the "tennis ball rule"). A kohlrabi with unwilted leaves still attached is undoubtedly fresh. If only large ones are available, peel away the tough outer layers before using.
TRICKS: The appearance of this unique edible is itself a trick! Plant a straight line of them on both sides of the walkway leading to your front door in midsummer (alternate red and white varieties), make a sign for Halloween that says "Follow the living spaceships to your Trick or Treat," then eat them at Thanksgiving.

1. A young kohlrabi plant, just beginning to develop the bulge that will become the distinctive above-ground corm.

2. Traditional green kohlrabi; pick all kohlrabis while they are still small for the best flavor.

3. If only large specimens are available, peel away the tough outer layers and use only the tender insides.

Opposite page: Red kohlrabi actually tends toward the purplish. Its vibrant color makes it an interesting choice in an otherwise ornamental patch. The large, rootlike body grows aboveground, showing off its color and unusual form to the fullest.

leeks

Are these European favorites giant scallions? Or leafy, upright onions without the distinctive round bulb? They are certainly the mildest-tasting of the alliums, easier to grow than onions, and a true gourmet treat for your "Continental" garden.

SCIENTIFIC NAME: *Allium porrum*

TYPES: The quick-to-mature varieties (Lincoln, rated at a speedy 50 days, and the classic early variety King Richard) are sometimes sown thickly and harvested tall, slender, and young in bunches, like scallions; these types are less cold-hardy than "real" leeks. Standard long-season leeks laugh at cold weather but take 110 to 130 days to achieve that impressive supermarket size. Some varieties have a pretty bluish hue to their leaves.

GROWING TIPS: In the North, plant in spring for fall harvest. In the South, plant in summer for winter pulling. Blanching produces much more of the clear white stalk preferred in cooking. Two ways to blanch the stalks like supermarket types: 1) Hill the soil up an extra inch around the growing plants three or four times during the growing season; or 2) Use a dibble to make deep (equal to about half the final plant size) planting holes, put your leek "starts" in the holes, but do not fill those holes back up with soil right away; just an inch to start, then add more soil gradually three or four times during the year (a technique known as "reverse hilling").

HARVEST: Leeks are delicious at any size, although arguably best when young—and always tastiest after the plants have endured a bit of frost. Harvest spring-sown crops after the first fall frost (the plants are very hardy); summer-sown in the South, anytime over the winter.

BUYING: Look for fresh leaves and plenty of white on the stalks.

STORAGE: Many gardeners mulch their plants well and pull as needed over winter. Otherwise, trim off the roots and all but a few green inches from the leaves ("flags") and they will keep for months in the fridge.

TRICKS: Leeks are not difficult to grow from seed, but starting with plants makes the blanching easier; larger garden centers and most specialty catalogues sell bunches of baby leeks that make such planting a snap.

1. Leek leaves are known as "flags" by allium aficionados.

2. The white section is the part most prized by chefs.

3. Use the greenish stalks as you would scallions.

4. Trim off these roots and the tops of the flags for long-term refrigerator storage.

Lettuce thrives in the crisp air of spring and fall, but when heat arrives, it sends up a big central seed stalk and turns bitter. Gardeners challenged by small spaces should grow lettuce early and late in the season, and use those plots for heat-loving plants in between.

SCIENTIFIC NAME: *Lactuca sativa*

TYPES: Loose-leaf lettuces do not form heads; their leaves can be harvested repeatedly when young (cut-and-come-again style) or left to grow large enough to cover the most enormous sandwich. The leaves of romaine (*cos*) tend to bunch together in distinctive style. The leaves of head lettuces (like the classic iceberg variety) curl around each other, forming a tight, round ball of overlapping leaves. The leaves of butterhead, Boston, and Bibb varieties form small heads surrounded by looser outer leaves.

GROWING TIPS: Start the first run or two of plants indoors and transplant out just before your last frost date in spring. Begin direct sowing as soon as the soil warms up enough to germinate the seeds. Start sowing fall crops when daytime temperatures drop below 80°.

HARVEST: Cut for gourmet "baby green" salads at the three-inch stage; the plants will regrow several runs of tasty leaves. Harvest heading lettuce before the weather gets too warm or the leaves will be bitter. (White milky sap at the cut stem is the sign that this has already occurred.)

BUYING: If heads are priced "by the each," get the heaviest. If by the pound, go for smaller heads, which will be tastier. If brown marks go deep, the lettuce is old. "Baby green mixes" should not look wilted. Colored lettuces are tastier and more nutritious than all-green varieties; dark green is better than light green; the blanched centers of head lettuces have little or no taste or nutrition.

STORAGE: In open plastic bags in the coldest part of your fridge; replace bags if they show obvious beads of moisture inside.

TRICKS: Sow a variety of colorful leaf lettuces thickly together and harvest premixed greens with scissors. The plants like being crowded, and their thick growth will prevent weeds.

1. Put started plants into the ground for your first spring crop; lettuce plants don't mind a chill, but cold weather prevents the seeds from germinating.

2. Loose-leaf types are favored by gardeners who like to pick a truly fresh garden salad every evening; unlike heading lettuces, these cut-and-come-again plants regrow their leaves after each cutting.

3. Some lettuces are "in betweeners"—loose outer leaves surrounding a loose head. Cut off some outer leaves for an early taste, or simply harvest the entire plant when small and young—when the taste is sweetest.

4. Lettuces that form nice, tight heads must be harvested whole; do this before the weather gets too warm, or the taste will be bitter.

The master class. These tropical delights of summer hide their sinfully sweet and juicy flesh behind coquettishly mysterious hard shells. Is the treasure inside *ripe?* Will it be *sweet?* What *color* is it in there? Not for the timid or space-challenged, melons demand faith, patience, precognition, more faith, and lots of room. But the reward of a ripe and perfect melon is well worth the emotional investment.

SCIENTIFIC NAME: *Cucumis melo*

TYPES: Those netted fruits with orange or green flesh you call cantaloupes are actually muskmelons, a name proven by their musky flavor and fragrance. (Eastern types are orange-skinned under their net; Western types are greenish underneath a heavier brown netting.) The hard rind of winter melons (including honeydews, casabas, and Crenshaws) makes them the best for storage; the skins can be white, pale green, or salmon pink, with green or orange flesh; very sweet, they lack their cousins' strong perfume. To taste a true cantaloupe, enjoy the ambrosial (and, some say, aphrodisiac) deep orange flesh of a French Charentais melon (smallish, with beautiful light-green or blue hard, smooth skin). But don't get cocky about these distinctions—thanks to selective (and accidental) breeding, there are many variations and mixed marriages out there.

GROWING TIPS: Melons like a lot of warmth and a long growing season. In the North, start the seeds indoors in large pots (they do not like to have their roots disturbed during transplanting) and do not put them out until all chance of cool weather is past.

HARVEST: Muskmelons will "slip" (pull away easily from the vine) when ripe. Otherwise, judge ripeness by days to maturity, smell, change in rind color, loss of color in the leaf closest to the fruit and/or a withering of the closest tendril. Research the ripeness cues for your types carefully; picking too late can taste just as bad as too soon.

BUYING: Judge muskmelons (American "cantaloupes") by smell. A ripe honeydew will have a glossy skin and "give" slightly at the blossom end.

STORAGE: Muskmelons in the fridge; winter melons in a cool, dry place. Always allow freshly picked Charentais and winter melons to sit out ("cure") for a few days.

TRICKS: Protect and warm young plants with row covers (see page 40) early in the season. Grow your vines trailing over rocks or stone to further increase warmth.

1. Summer melons often have powerful scents and flavors.

2. The greenish skin under the heavy netting reveals that this is a Western type of muskmelon (not a cantaloupe). Its Eastern cousin—opposite—is orange-skinned beneath its somewhat finer netting.

3. The sensuous seed cavity of a charentais melon is a true cantaloupe.

4. Is it ripe? Look to the tendril closest to the fruit for the answer. This one is still firm and fresh-looking. When it is dried and brown, the adjacent melon is likely to be ready.

French for "mixture," this combination of young and pretty leaf lettuces and small, tasty spring greens like arugula, mizuna, and radicchio looks even better growing in the garden than tossed in your salad bowl. Grow mesclun just the way you buy it in the supermarket—all mixed together! Simply sow a bed thickly with several different varieties of greens (many of which are actually a brilliant red) and harvest cut-and-come-again style daily with scissors. Your own mixed organic baby greens—fresher than the market and at a fraction of the cost.

TYPES: Begin with a mixture of colorful lettuces —bright reds, distinctive greens, bicolors, bronzes, and freckles—with frilly, ruffled, oak leaf, deer's tongue, and other interesting-to-look-at leaves. Potential spicy components include (from most to least hot): mustard greens, arugula (aka roquette or rocket), cress (broadleaf or curly cress—peppergrass, not watercress, which *is* hot but needs to grow in a very wet area), komatsuna ("mustard spinach"), mizuna (aka kyona) and mibuna. Other leafy greens often include endive, radicchio, chicory (red- and green-leafed varieties), spinach, chervil, mâche ("corn salad," a popular European spring green), vegetable (not grain) amaranth (very colorful and nutritious), tatsoi (a dark-green Asian green), and the fancier-leafed and colored kales.

GROWING TIPS: Although you *can* grow the ingredients separately, they look wonderfully ornamental when mixed (and harvested) together. Sow your first bed as soon as the soil can be worked in spring, then plant a fresh run every two weeks. Although almost all of the components are cool-weather-lovers, you can stretch the season a bit by planting late-spring runs in some shade and watering often.

HARVEST: With scissors, when leaves are two to three inches high. You should be able to get at least three or four cuttings from each run.

BUYING: Avoid mixes whose components look wilted or whose tiny stalks are browning. The smaller the leaves the better.

STORAGE: Cut only as much as you need if homegrown (harvest right into a salad spinner). Store-bought: In an open plastic bag in the crisper; change the bag and add a paper towel if the leaves are excessively moist from misting.

TRICKS: Most seed companies offer a variety of premixed mescluns, each containing a nice variety—just sow, add water, and eat!

1. Harvest your premixed salad with scissors when the leaves are three inches high. Take only what you will use that day, and always cut the highest growth.

2. A nice mix of colorful leaf lettuces is the heart of a great mesclun.

3. Look for crisp individual components and smallish leaves when you buy mesclun in stores.

4. Look for interesting leaf shapes and textures as well as a wide range of colors when you choose the plants for your mesclun mix.

Well beyond easy-to-grow, most members of this diverse family can be downright invasive and should be watched carefully (or grown in containers) if you want a mixed garden and not a mint farm. But the rewards are worth your vigilance: The leaves are extremely useful for cooking and medicinal use, and most are so fragrant that just rustling a plant creates instant aromatherapy. The small flowers can be very colorful, and attract hordes of pollinators and other beneficial insects to the garden.

SCIENTIFIC NAME: *Mentha* species Lemon balm (*Melissa officinalis*) is also considered a member of the mint family.

TYPES: Peppermint leaves make a fine garnish or calming tea. Spearmint provides the classic mint jelly/mint julep leaf. Lime, apple, pineapple (variegated, with lovely white edging), chocolate, and orange mints impart their distinctive namesake flavors, and, except for apple, are among the least aggressive types. Very low-growing (half-inch) Corsican mint has a light peppermint flavor and makes an attractive, aromatic ground cover. Lemon balm produces huge amounts of citrus-flavored leaves that can be substituted for lemon peel in recipes, used to add a lemon flavor to food and drink, made into a refreshing tea or tied up in a porous bag and infused into a warm bath to lift the spirits.

GROWING TIPS: *Mentha* mints rarely come true from seed; planting cuttings or root divisions yields the best results.

HARVEST: Continually, with scissors, to prevent flowering; in the morning or late evening for finest flavor and highest essential-oil content. For a more ornamental appearance and/or to attract beneficial insects and butterflies, let flower, then prune gently to the desired shape.

BUYING: Scent is all; choose with your nose.

STORAGE: Hang in loose bunches to dry, or strip leaves off the thick stems and freeze tightly packed in heavy plastic.

TIPS: Do not underestimate the aggressiveness of these plants: Spearmint, apple mint, and lemon balm are especially troublesome if not contained! Allow mints to flower near plants that require pollination, such as squash, or that tend to suffer insect attack; or simply to attract butterflies.

1. Peppermint plants provide the perfect leaves to brew up in a tea to soothe a troubled stomach.

2. The trees that bear the beans that create real chocolate require an intensely tropical clime, but you can grow this chocolate-flavored mint just about anywhere.

3. Lemon balm. The leaves of this aggressive grower make an excellent mosquito repellent. Simply rub the crushed, fresh leaves on exposed skin at sunset.

4. Catnip, an ancient herbal cure and perhaps an even more ancient feline fun provoker.

Opposite page: Frequent cutting and/or pinching back the developing buds will deliver leaves of superior flavor, but will deny you the sight of these pretty flowers. For the best of both worlds, grow two patches—one for leaves, one for blooms to attract butterflies and beneficial insects.

Although mushrooms are not plants in any sense of the word, these fungi *do* grow, and many are edible. You would have to study diligently and learn identification perfectly to safely harvest edible mushrooms (like prized morels) in the wild. ("There are *old* mushroom hunters and there are *bold* mushroom hunters—but there are no *old, bold* mushroom hunters.") Instead, harvest perfectly safe gourmet eating—*indoors*—with mushroom-growing kits. Spores of edible mushrooms are combined with their preferred growing medium (often sawdust) in a bag, and come complete with detailed instructions. Growing these delicacies is not quite as easy as "just add water," but it comes close.

SCIENTIFIC NAMES AND TYPES: Prized for both its flavor and medicinal properties, the shiitake mushroom (*Lentinula edodes*) grows in sawdust; a typical kit will produce eight to ten meal-size harvests. Several types of oyster mushrooms (*Pleurotus* species) are available in kits, including the wildly colored "pink" or "flamingo" oyster (*P. djamor*) and the "espresso" variety (*P. ostreatus*), whose preferred growing medium is spent coffee grounds! Although we think of the prized portobello (*Agaricus blazei*) only as a tasty edible, other cultures also value it for its reputed health-enhancing properties.
GROWING TIPS: If you are not limited to indoor growing, you can obtain kits or spawn that allow you to cultivate "wild" mushrooms like *morels* (*Morchella angusticeps*) and King Stropharia (The Garden Giant; *Stropharia rugoso-annulata*), which can take two years to produce delicious giants weighing several pounds apiece!
HARVEST: Frequently; almost all kits produce numerous sequential "flushes," and removing the current crop promptly will spark the growth of the next round.
BUYING: Look for firmness and definition; mushrooms shrink and brown at the edges as they age.
STORAGE: Unless otherwise instructed, at cool room temperature, away from direct light.
TRICKS: Some types (including shiitakes, oysters, and portobellos) will continue to produce mushrooms after the kit is "exhausted" if you place the spent materials on wood chips, logs, or a compost pile (as directed in the instructions) outdoors.

1. A fully grown flush of shiitakes, ready for harvest. These popular mushrooms are prized equally by gourmet diners for their flavor and natural medicine enthusiasts for their health-enhancing properties.

2. Young oyster mushrooms emerge from their kit.

3. Fully grown "oysters"; these can reach a very large size and still be tender.

4. A pair of portobellos.

Opposite page: The portobello's geometric frills.

Although wonderfully edible, mustard looks as though it belongs in an ornamental bed rather than the kitchen garden. The plants begin life as stunningly beautiful little green-, purple-, and red-leafed wonders—ideal for adding spice to mesclun mixes and sandwiches, or used sparingly (they can be *really* hot) as "surprises" in a salad. As the greens grow taller, their colors become more intense, showing off the crinkles and frills of the leaf shape to spectacular effect. Then up comes a central stalk, which produces first a flush of lovely yellow flowers (those uncultivated yellow fields you often see from the roadside are wild mustards), and then the seeds that give this underutilized treasure its name. Yes, mustard seeds. And yes, you can grind them to make your own condiment—which will be much more flavorful than store-bought.

SCIENTIFIC NAME: *Brassica juncea.* Thought to be a wild hybrid of *B. rapa* (bok-choy, Chinese cabbage, turnips, etc.) and *B. nigra* (black mustard, a European native whose seeds were once predominant in most table mustards).

TYPES: Regular or "giant"-sized leaves; red, green, or purple (individually) leafed; variegated color varieties; and frilly, flat, or crinkly. Mizuna and tatsoi, components of many mesclun mixes, are true mustards—the former an extremely frilly type, the latter a mild-tasting spinach look-alike.

GROWING TIPS: Frost-hardy and heat-tolerant (an unusual but welcome combination of attributes), mustards are ridiculously easy to grow. Plant a few in every bed for tasty picking and ornamentation—and increased attraction of pollinators when they flower.

HARVEST: Small leaves tend to have the best flavor; large ones (often dramatically so on "giant mustard" types) can be *very* spicy, rivaling hot peppers. Harvest leaves before the plants set seed. Collect mustard seed by shaking the plant heads over large sheets of white paper after the flowers have come and gone.

BUYING: Not often found outside of spicy mesclun mixes; but if you do, choose the smallest leaves for best flavor.

TRICKS: Plants readily self-seed, and those seeds will survive winter to sprout on their own the following spring. Place especially colorful varieties in ornamental beds; the huge crinkled green-and-purple leaves of Red Giant are especially striking.

1. The lovely yellow flowers of mustard . . .

2. . . . become seed pods . . .

3. . . . that produce the vital ingredient for a very familiar sandwich spread. Grow and grind your own!

You can buy onions cheaply at the store, and the quality is often very good—but there is a world of delicious and colorful varieties out there known only to those who grow their own.

SCIENTIFIC NAME: *Allium cepa*

TYPES: Red, yellow, or white in color. Sweet ("mild," "slicing") onions, like the legendary (and geographically proprietary) Vidalia and Walla Walla varieties, lack sulfur and pungency; delicious fresh, they do not store well. Storage onions have much more of a bite, and keep well for long periods of time. Long-day varieties are bred to be grown in the North; in the South, short-day varieties are more reliable. (The "wrong" type may not bulb up properly.) Most short-day onions are sweet.

GROWING TIPS: Sweet onions can be grown using seed (planted in the fall in the South and spring in the North) or bunches of scallionlike young plants. Storage onions can be grown from seed, plants, or "sets"—tiny onions that are the result of seeds being crowded together a year earlier. All onions—especially sweet—require a lot of water during the season to keep them from tasting overly "hot."

HARVEST: When some of the leaves fall over, knock the rest down (to keep rain water out of their necks). A week later, pull the whole crop out of the ground and cure (dry) for a few days.

BUYING: Reject onions that feel soft anywhere, especially toward the top. More papery layers of skin are better than fewer, and small, tight necks are better than big, loose ones.

STORAGE: Use sweet onions promptly, or chop and freeze for later use. Make sure storage onions are completely dry, then store braided or in mesh ("onion") bags at high humidity (70 percent) and low temperature (just above freezing). While onions keep well in the fridge, they will sprout if apples or other fruit are also kept there.

TRICKS: If an onion sprouts in storage, slice it open carefully to remove (and use) just the outer layers. Then plant the rooted, scallionlike remainder; it will grow into a large onion.

1. Many gardeners feel they get the best results from planting onion "sets"; these mini-onions are the result of seeds being deliberately crowded together a year earlier.

2. When the first sproutlike "tops" fall over, knock the rest down. Otherwise, rainwater may collect in the tops and rot the onions below.

3. The distinctive donut shape of flat Italian cipollini onions; these are among the best-tasting.

4. Pick onions young and use as scallions.

Opposite page: Or allow them to grow and develop that distinctive large, full root.

Gardeners who thought they had been growing oregano for years often learn they actually have its milder-flavored (but much more hardy) cousin, wild marjoram. Even the best reference books disagree on the distinctions between these and similar members of this branch of the mint family—even on just which plant the Greeks first called "joy from the mountains." *And* they cross-pollinate and regress so readily that seeds can rarely be trusted to produce the plant claimed on the package. But all members of the family are edible, and all are excellent choices for flavoring Italian-style dishes, especially tomato sauces and most especially pizza. Start with a plant whose taste you enjoy and you will not be disappointed.

SCIENTIFIC NAMES AND TYPES: All oreganos and marjorams fall into the *Origanum* genus (sometimes called *Majorana*). The easily confused common oregano and wild marjoram are both *O. vulgare.* The elusive, highly sought, strongly flavored Greek oregano ("pizza herb") may be labeled as the subspecies *hirtum* or given its own classification as *O. heracleoticum.* No matter the name, it is a very tender perennial that will not survive winter north of USDA Zone 7. True ("sweet") marjoram may be called *O. majorana* or *O.* or *M. hortensis*; whatever you call it, it is as strongly flavored as Greek oregano and even less cold hardy. (If an oregano-like plant survives winter in the North, it is likely wild marjoram; the others are perennial only in warm climes.)

GROWING TIPS: If you like surprises, start with seeds. Otherwise, select the largest plant with the strongest aroma and place it where it will have room to spread. The more it smells like oregano, the less likely it will survive winter in the northern half of the United States. In Zone 6 and lower, pot up Greek oregano and sweet marjoram, and bring them inside for the winter.

HARVEST: Frequently—at least weekly—with scissors to prevent flowering (or pinch the growing tips back, which will also make it bushier).

BUYING: Judge by the strength of its smell.

TRICKS: Beg, borrow—or yes, *steal* (if you must) a few sprigs from any oregano-like plants you encounter that have a really strong aroma. You may never see their like again. Root the cuttings in water and then plant them in your own garden.

1. Is it oregano? Or wild marjoram? Only the plants' ability to survive winter in non-Mediterranean climes will tell the tale for sure.

2. Harvest frequently to prevent flowers like these from forming. As the plants grow in size, cut and pinch to coax them into a more bushy shape.

3. Save old spice jars for use when you dry your own—much tastier—crop.

Opposite page: Fine flavor or attracting beneficial insects? You must choose—this plant will soon look beautiful, but the flavor will be inferior.

Parsley has a lot to recommend its being actually eaten. Ounce for ounce, it is one of the most nutrition-packed foods, containing as much vitamin C and more vitamin A than broccoli. In its second (and final) year of life, this true biennial will produce an attractive flush of umbelliferous flowers (numerous tiny blooms that, together, form an umbrella-like shape).

SCIENTIFIC NAME: *Petroselinum crispum*
TYPES: Flat leaf (Italian) varieties provide the most flavor; curled leaf types are the prettiest; and root types (sometimes called Hamburg, actually the name of the best-known variety of this type) produce large edible white parsniplike roots prized for their nutty, peppery flavor, cooked or raw. (Old recipes for borscht generally specify Hamburg roots as an essential ingredient.)
GROWING TIPS: The seed has a deserved reputation for being very slow to germinate. To help matters along, place the seed in a cloth bag and dip it in and out of a bowl of lukewarm water for two hours (while you watch a movie on TV), then plant the seeds outdoors and they will sprout. You must dip; if you just soak the seeds, none of them will sprout. And do not try starting the plants indoors—the roots are very fussy about transplanting. Once the plants are up, keep the soil moist and all will be well.
HARVEST: Wait until the leaves are nice and large; there is no danger of this biennial plant flowering the first year. Harvest through the winter in mild climes (parsley prefers cool weather to hot). Harvest leaves of root types very sparingly—if at all—then dig up the roots after the first frost.
BUYING: Look for crisp, unwilted leaves, without brown on the stems.
STORAGE: Cut long stalks and store upright in tall glass jars with a little water in the coldest part of the fridge. Dry leaves quickly (in a food dryer or oven set low) for long-term storage; do not hang to dry or the leaves will turn yellow. Store roots like carrots.
TRICKS: Plant curly-leaf varieties in the ornamental garden. Grow some plants indoors on a sunny windowsill for nutritious winter greens and breath freshening. Allow some plants to remain in place for their second year so they can produce their beneficial insect-attracting (and highly ornamental) flowers.

1. Nature's breath freshener. A few well-chewed sprigs can erase even the evidence of recent garlic consumption.

2. Flavorful flat leaf parsley.

3. Extra-fancy and ornamental curly leaf parsley.

Opposite page: Hamburg, a unique type of parsley grown for its tasty roots rather than for its leaves.

Peas are like opera; the potential for tragedy lurks in every scene. Plant the big seeds too early and they will rot in the cold, wet ground; plant too late and hot weather will shrivel the vines before any pods even form. No, "peaing" is *not* for the timid—but the reward for success is an incomparable springtime treat.

SCIENTIFIC NAME: *Pisum sativum*

TYPES: The classic "peas in a pod" are called shelling, garden, or English peas. Snap peas, like the prototypical Sugar Snap variety, are a recent development, bred to be eaten pod and all. (See page 136 for Snow Peas.)

WARNING: The poisonous and badly named "sweet pea" garden flower (*Lathyrus odoratus*) is *not* edible in any form.

GROWING TIPS: Peas require a slightly alkaline ("sweet") soil; if your garden tends toward the acidic, add a small amount of wood ash or lime. Be sure to get your crop in the ground by April 1. Provide a fence, trellis, or long branches for the vines to climb. Peas like to be crowded; sow the seed thickly, especially in warm climes—the plants will help shade the soil. To try for a *fall* crop, plant in a shady spot three months before frost and have covers ready in the autumn to protect the plants against hard frost.

HARVEST: Shelling: When the peas inside the pod are nicely plump, zip open the convenient built-in string and collect the tender morsels inside. Snap: Let the peas inside develop a nice bulge, "snap" the pod off the plant, zip off the string, and eat the rest, pod and all.

BUYING: Scour farm markets mid to late June for shelling peas; if they taste sweet, buy in bulk and freeze. Snap peas should be crisp and green; reject limp or browning specimens.

STORAGE: Snap peas are best eaten fresh; refrigerate promptly or they become limp. Shelled English peas freeze wonderfully in heavy plastic containers, or "can" them in a pressure cooker.

TRICKS: Pre-sprout pea seed in damp paper towels for a few days before planting in spring; the seeds will not germinate in cold soil, but the sprouted plants do not mind chill weather. Add "pea and bean inoculant" when you plant—available at larger garden centers, these nitrogen-fixing bacteria colonize the roots of your plants (forming visible galls), creating a symbiotic relationship that allows the peas to take plant-feeding nitrogen directly from the air.

1. Shelling peas, also called English or garden peas. Just the sweet seeds will be eaten.

2. Always provide a sturdy support for your pea vines to clamber up.

3. Snap peas. Zip off the string and eat the rest.

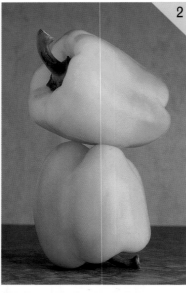

Never call these beauties "green peppers." All sweet peppers will ripen to a beautiful final color—red, orange, yellow, or chocolate (sorry, you only get the color, not the flavor). Sometimes there is a handsome purple stage in between. (Purple peppers are better than green ones, but are still not fully ripe.) The distinctive "bite" of green ones comes from starches that will turn to sugars as the color changes, releasing their true flavor and increasing their nutritional benefits tenfold.

SCIENTIFIC NAME: *Capsicum annuum.* A double misnomer, as sweet peppers completely lack the capsaicin that gives hot peppers their fiery spice, and the plants are long-lived perennials if protected from freezing (although most Americans *do* grow them as annuals).

TYPES: Final fruit colors include red, orange, yellow, and a rich chocolate brown. The classic, blocky supermarket shape is called a *bell pepper*; these are generally the largest and takes the longest to mature. *Lipstick* is the prettiest of the smaller, easier-to-grow *apple*, or *top-shaped* peppers. *Italian*, *banana*, or *frying peppers* (like the heirloom Corno di Toro, a long, curvy work of art) are elongated. *Miniature peppers*, like Jingle Bells, are tiny, bell-shaped, and fast to mature; a typical plant may produce 50 or more bite-sized beauties. The term "pimiento" is used for a number of sweet varieties, some of which are dried and finely ground to make the familiar spice paprika—at least in the United States; true paprika is prepared only from specific Hungarian and Romanian sweet varieties that have a touch of heat. The "black pepper" on our tables does not come from peppers—it is ground from the dried "corns" (fruits) of an unrelated tropical plant.

GROWING TIPS: Start with big plants and keep them warm early in the season; peppers dislike cool weather.

HARVEST: After their colors change—never while green. Always *cut* peppers free; pulling them off can injure the plant.

BUYING: Fully ripe peppers have a short shelf life. Select shiny, blemish-free fruits.

STORAGE: In open plastic bags in the fridge. Sweet peppers also dry and freeze well.

TRICKS: Grow some compact varieties in pots and bring them indoors for the winter; the plants will last many, many seasons.

1. A pepper plant in flower. Look closely and you can see the small fruit that has replaced a previous bloom.

2. The top member of this yellow team still displays a bit of green.

3. A green pepper turns to an in-between hue of purple on the journey to its final, ripe color.

4. These fully ripened slices have developed their true flavor and nutritional value.

Opposite page: When ripe, that "green pepper" will turn red—or perhaps orange, or yellow.

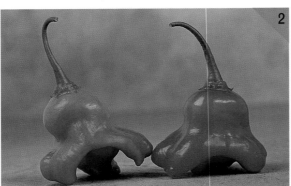

Almost unlimited in their range of shapes and colors, hot peppers are *the* most ornamental of the edibles. The plants have a wonderful upright habit, the fruits are magnificently colorful, and their culinary uses are almost endless.

SCIENTIFIC NAMES AND TYPES: *Capsicum annuum* includes the (medium hot) jalapeños; chiltepins ("bird peppers"—immune to the intense heat of the small, berrylike fruits, birds spread the seed); highly ornamental varieties like Ordono (opposite page; these fiery hot, Christmas-light-shaped fruits progress through green, white, purple, yellow, and orange stages before reaching ripe redness); and the rudely shaped Peter Pepper. *C. baccatum* (Aji) are very hot South American peppers that come in a huge diversity of shapes, from tiny marbles and bullets to long, thin chiles, little hats, bells, and even orchid-shaped fruits. *C. chinense* (another bad name—these dangerously hot peppers are originally from the Amazon, not Asia) includes Scotch bonnets and the hottest of all peppers— the famous habanero—which should be handled with *extreme* caution. *C. frutescens* includes Tabasco (named for the town in Mexico where it was discovered) and other very hot varieties. *C. pubescens* types, like the apple-shaped rocoto, have purple flowers, black seeds, thick skins, and hairy leaves. There are also many wild varieties and crosses—including sweet peppers that look just like chiles and hot-as-blazes ones disguised as innocent sweet bell peppers (Mexi-Bell is a very hot bell pepper look-alike especially loved by pranksters).

GROWING TIPS: Same as for sweet peppers.

HARVEST: Unlike sweet peppers, chiles should be harvested and sampled at every color stage; the taste and potential uses change with the hues.

BUYING: Same as for sweet peppers.

TRICKS: Keep handsome specimens in pots and treat like houseplants. Grind dried fruits to make a hot pepper shake. Process fresh fruits with vinegar in a blender to make hot sauce.

WARNING: *Always wash your hands after touching hot peppers! Chant: "I will not touch my face" repeatedly while working with them in the kitchen.* Milk is the only antidote for foolish gourmet bravery; hold the liquid in your mouth until the fire goes out.

1. The classic chile pepper look.

2. Hot peppers come in all shapes, colors, and sizes. This one resembles a bell in both its green (immature) and red (ripe) stages. The tastes of these two will be very different.

3. The shape of many hot peppers makes them perfect additions to an otherwise purely ornamental garden.

4. Habaneros (meaning from Havana) are the hottest peppers known. These distinctively shaped fruits register more units of heat on the research-based Scoville scale than any other. Ordinary (orange when ripe) habaneros rate a fiery 300,000 units (about 50 times hotter than a jalapeño), and the Red Savina variety—the single hottest pepper ever tested by far—rates a blistering 577,000 units. Handle *all* habaneros with extreme caution!!!

If you have never grown your own potatoes, you have never really tasted one. To experience the swanlike reality of this garden ugly duckling, dig up a perfect young spud, rinse it off, and bite into it right there in the garden, like the first ripe tomato of summer. Juice will run down your face as you experience a sweetness that left storage potatoes long ago.

SCIENTIFIC NAME: *Solanum tuberosum*

TYPES: Yellow-fleshed varieties, like the naturally buttery "Yukon Gold," are the best-tasting, followed by the redskins. Blue and purple potatoes are genetically closer to the original tuber (native to Peru) from which the familiar white potato was bred, but their taste is inferior (use them to make a red, white, and blue potato salad for the Fourth of July). Whites and reds tend to be the most productive.

GROWING TIPS: Bury small *whole* potatoes with visible "eye" sprouts (do not cut them into pieces first) six inches deep and a foot apart. After the firm green shoots break through the ground, mulch the area deeply. Keep mulching throughout the season; the tubers creep upward, but *must* be kept *completely* in the dark to prevent unhealthy (greenish-colored) alkaloid compounds from forming in the skin and flesh.

HARVEST: Mark the date flowers appear on top of the plants (those blooms reflect the color of the tubers below). A month later, you can pull up the plants to harvest tender "new" potatoes— small in size, but rich in flavor. Otherwise, wait until the above-ground growth dies.

BUYING: Reject loose potatoes in favor of ones tucked safely away inside heavy paper (not clear plastic) bags; even ambient store light can cause those greenish alkaloids to form.

STORAGE: Keep perfect ones in a *dark,* cool, dry spot; you may gently brush off big chunks of dirt, but wait until you are ready to use to wash them. Damaged ones: Wash, cut away any bad parts (harvest injury, green color, etc.), slice what is left and store in lidded glass jars filled with cold water in the fridge; they will stay crisp for weeks—without a hint of browning.

TRICK: Ruth Stout's no-dig harvest: Rough up some soil with a garden fork, place seed potatoes on *top* of the dirt, and cover with plenty of straw. As the plants grow, continually pile on more straw. At the end of the season, push the straw aside and pick a bumper crop—right off the top of the soil!

1. Potato planting time. Plant small whole ones, not pieces.

2. Harvest time! If the soil is loose, pull up the plant gently; many of the tubers will remain attached to the roots. Search the surrounding soil carefully for stragglers.

3. A potato all sprouted and ready to plant.

4. Both these sprouts and later flowers reflect the color of the potato's skin and flesh.

Pumpkins have a well-deserved reputation for being space hogs. Their long vines like to wander, and they never seem to tire of "running." But if you have the room, there is no better way to use it; their enormous flowers and colorful fruits always bring a smile.

SCIENTIFIC NAMES AND TYPES: All pumpkins are squash, but not all squash are pumpkins. *Cucurbita pepo* is a large family that includes zucchini, gourds, and many pumpkins. Among the pumpkins are the charming "mini" (one pound each) varieties like Baby Bear and Jack Be Little, and some of the best Jack-o'-Lantern and pie varieties. *C. pepo* varieties are generally best eaten fresh. *C. maxima* (huge, "hairy" leaves) includes a number of winter squashes and monster-size pumpkins like Dill's Atlantic Giant (the largest of which has reached 1,000 pounds); its normal-size pumpkin family members (like the beautiful heirloom *Rouge Vif d'Etampes* or Cinderella pumpkin) are said to have the best taste. *C. moschata* family includes butternut squash and most of the cheese-wheel shaped pumpkins; this type stores well and loves long, hot summers. Lumina and other "white" varieties are orange inside but have a ghostly rind when ripe.

GROWING TIPS: Pumpkins have a "hollow leg" and will gleefully accept all the food and water you can provide. If space is tight, grow them upward, perhaps trellising the vines into trees.

HARVEST: Preferably when fully ripe and fairly hard. But most types will continue to ripen inside if picked a little green. Always cut the fruit cleanly away from the vine, and leave a good amount of stem attached to the fruit.

BUYING: Look for good color and avoid fruits with nicks or soft spots; scarring is fine if the rind there is hard. For pie or soup making, use a variety with the words "pie" or "sugar" in the name.

STORAGE: Pumpkins are winter squash; most undamaged specimens will store well into the next year in a cool (50°–60°) dry spot. "Cure" first by leaving out for a few days.

TRICKS: Whether you grow or purchase your pumpkins for carving, food, or fun, be sure to dry, season, and savor the seeds—they are the most nutritious part!

1. Pumpkin flowers can be huge—and tasty. They are as edible as any other squash flower.

2. A perfect pumpkin. Carve it. Bake the shell for pies. Toast the seeds. Or simply admire its perfection.

3. If vine borers are a problem in your region, grow one of the cheese-wheel-shaped varieties; their stems are solid, not hollow, and the pests cannot burrow into them.

4. "Mini" pumpkins are a delightful addition to any garden—especially one for children. Just be aware that only the fruits are miniature; the vines are often full-size.

5. Pumpkins—even medium-sized ones—grow on enormous vines.

Opposite page: "Spooky" white-when-ripe pumpkins are perfect for Halloween.

Supremely cold-hardy, radishes are often the first and last crops to be planted and picked in spring and fall. (They do not enjoy growing in summer's heat.) And they come in a surprisingly ornamental variety of shapes and colors.

SCIENTIFIC NAME: *Raphanus sativus*

TYPES: Some are hot and spicy, some are very mild. Spring (early) radishes mature in 22 to 30 days; the standard small round red globe also comes in white and violet colors (often sold mixed as "Easter Egg"), while the elongated (cylindrical) types range from pink-and-white (Shunkyo) to the beautiful French Breakfast— bright red on top and white on the bottom. Although not as common in stores as the round varieties, the elongated types are considered the best-tasting. Fall (winter, or storage) radishes take 50 to 60 days to mature and come in practically every shape and color, from the huge one-pound roots of Black Spanish (dark purple on the outside, white on the inside) to the beautiful variegated rose-colored interior of Misato Rose to the familiar long, white daikons, which are true radishes. Also a true radish, the odd European heirloom variety "rattail" grows four feet tall and produces foot-long edible pods that may have been used as the first "beer nuts."

GROWING TIPS: Sow multiple runs of spring varieties, and pay close attention—they come up and mature *fast*. The farther South you are, the more you should avoid summer growing; the roots get woody in the heat. Sow fall storage crops in August and September.

HARVEST: Use a calendar for early crops—if the package says 22 days, that is when to pick; just a few extra days in the ground can cause a woody, pithy taste to develop in spring types. (Radishes are edible as soon as they sprout.) Harvest storage radishes after the first frost.

BUYING: In spring, look for small roots—a sign that they were picked on time. Pay more attention to the freshness of the greens than to minor imperfections in the roots themselves. In fall, check for firmness; big size is okay.

STORAGE: Eat most of your spring radishes as soon as possible; store the rest in the fridge. Cut the tops off fall radishes and store in a cool, dry place; they will maintain good eating quality until the first spring crops are ready.

TRICKS: Sow twice as thickly as necessary and eat the sproutlike thinnings—which are spicy-hot and delicious. The leaves are edible as well; make a radish-only springtime salad of sliced roots atop washed greens!

1. Early radishes, sown as soon as the soil warms in spring, are ready to eat in just a few weeks.

2. Weeds are a radish's worst enemy.

3. The classic kitchen garden variety French Breakfast is beautiful and delicious. The smaller plants up front are the next run, planted two weeks after the first.

4. Although the pods are most impressive on the famed Rattail variety, all radishes will eventually produce flowers and then edible seedpods. All portions of the plant are edible at all stages.

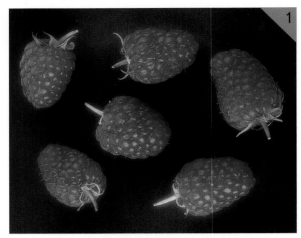

These intensely flavored berries are arguably the easiest fruits you can grow—so easy, in fact, that care must be taken in placing your patch or you will soon be displaced by a raspberry forest. Most varieties provide home growers with two full crops a year. *And* you only need to plant them *once*.

SCIENTIFIC NAME: *Rubus idaeus*

TYPES: Most ripen to a deep red or gold color (sometimes called yellow, these supremely sweet varieties actually take on a pinkish blush when dead ripe). Summer bearers produce their crop only on second-year canes (green shoots emerge in spring, grow all season, rest over winter, produce flowers and fruits the following summer, and then are done). Fall bearers (or everbearers) produce two crops: Green shoots emerge in spring, grow all summer, and then flower and fruit at their very tips just as fall arrives. The canes then turn brown over winter, but produce new shoots up and down their length early the following spring that bear large crops of berries just as summer approaches; then those canes are done.

GROWING TIPS: Raspberries need only good drainage to be happy; feel free to banish them to your poorest growing area, where they can run free to their invasive hearts' content. More new shoots emerge in spring than anyone needs; the best patches begin with these extras from a nearby grower. Trellis them if you like, but remove only completely spent canes—do not cut everbearing patches to the ground each year, or you will cut your harvest in half. Although the plants require a winter chill, a handful of varieties can be grown successfully in the South.

HARVEST: If the fruits resist a gentle tug, they are not yet ripe; pick only when they slip easily from their canes.

BUYING: Examine packages very carefully—raspberries do not travel well. Vented plastic is better than paperboard. Either way, reject any with stains on the bottom.

STORAGE: Eat golden ones immediately; they simply do not keep. Place red ones in vented plastic in the fridge, or freeze perfect ones in heavy, lidded plastic containers.

TRICKS: When harvest is at its peak, process big batches in a blender, freeze in pint-size plastic containers, and use in winter to replace some of the liquid in chocolate cake recipes—The Million Dollar Dessert!

1. Delicious and ultranutritious red raspberries; second only to blueberries in naturally occurring antioxidants.

2. Golden raspberry canes are much better behaved than those of red varieties; the berries are also more delicate in nature—and sweeter.

3. Heritage. These beautiful berries produce two crops each season.

Opposite page: Raspberry flowers precede the delicious fruit.

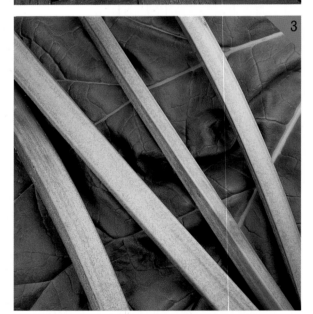

The only true vegetable we use like a fruit, this relative of buckwheat is highly unusual. How did anyone ever figure out how to eat this herbaceous perennial with poisonous leaves safely? Ah, but remove those leaves, sweeten the stems with sugar, bake in a tasty crust, and you will have created a unique seasonal treat many gardeners *require* to believe that spring really has arrived.

SCIENTIFIC NAME: *Rheum x cultorum*

TYPES: Although it has a few ornamental cousins, there is only one type—available in only a handful of varieties. (Although rhubarb chard looks surprisingly like its namesake, it is a true chard, and completely unrelated.)

GROWING TIPS: Root divisions planted in rich soil in the fall will produce a few edible stems the following spring, and many more each year thereafter. Ask a local rhubarb grower for some to get started; the plants *must* be divided every five years or they will stop producing. The farther North you are, the more rhubarb will enjoy growing in your garden. Mid-Southerners should provide some shade and plenty of water in summertime. Although it is *possible* that some varieties (Cherry; Cherry Red) may produce in the Deep South, it is smarter simply to buy "imported" stalks in the store.

HARVEST: After the stalks turn from green to red; pull them away at the base of the plant by twisting them off—do not cut with a knife. Remove every last bit of the poisonous leaf, then use the stalks as you would any fruit.

BUYING: Look for large, firm red stems with no trace of green.

STORAGE: The stems will keep in a plastic bag in the fridge for up to a week. They can also be chopped into inch-long pieces, placed in a heavy sealed plastic container, and frozen for out-of-season enjoyment.

TRICKS: Consider growing as a leafy ornamental; the red stalks are highly attractive. If flowers appear, remove them promptly; they are not very attractive, the seeds probably will not germinate (and if they do, probably will not produce usable rhubarb), and they sap the strength of the plant. But always leave a few leafy shoots alone each season so that the roots can collect and store energy for the following year's crop.

1. Remove *all* the leaf; eat only leafless stem material.

2. Rhubarb chard looks like rhubarb but tastes very different.

3. If this is all the store has to offer, do not buy. You want red, not green.

4. Halfway to the ultimate taste of summer—rhubarb pie!

Essential in cooking, rosemary is also *truly* "the herb of remembrance"; its naturally occurring compounds stimulate our senses, banish fatigue, and improve memory. (Take fresh sprigs on long drives and inhale deeply to combat drowsiness.) Plant as an annual if that is all your climate allows. In the South, allow to grow into its natural large, shrublike shape.

SCIENTIFIC NAME: *Rosmarinus* species

TYPES: The standard shrub-size plant *(R. officinalis)* and a ground cover "prostrate" variety *(R. lavendulaceus)* with inferior flavor. Most rosemarys produce tiny bluish-purple flowers in fall, (some bloom every year—some never). Numerous varieties are available, including ARP, which is bred to be especially cold hardy.

GROWING TIPS: These plants will happily survive the winter in a protected area (near a house or in a corner wall) in a Zone 6 *city,* but die a few miles away sitting out in the open. They thrive in Zone 7 and above. Always start with plants; rosemary *can* be grown from seed, but neither you nor the plants will be happy with the result most of the time.

HARVEST: Anytime, as needed, cutting entire branches. Harvesting gradually over the course of the season allows you to shape the bush into a pleasing design; the dusky, dark-green needles are highly ornamental.

BUYING: By smell! If the aroma is not intense and stimulating, move on.

STORAGE: Tricky. Rosemary is best used fresh. In season, harvest as needed on a daily basis. Zone 7 and warmer, harvest shrublike plants sparsely through the winter and heavily in season. Otherwise, place individual cut branches/ stems in a tall jar with a few inches of water in the bottom, keep in a cool spot or in the fridge, and strip the needles as needed. Freeze whole branches in heavy plastic; do not strip the needles first; you will lose a lot of the powerful essential oils.

TRICKS: In the North, grow in a big pot and move it outdoors in the summer and into your coolest bright indoor area in the winter. Heat a griddle, pour in your best olive oil, and when the oil is hot, add freshly dug sliced new potatoes; sear for a few minutes, turn once, toss in more fresh rosemary than you think you should, cook for another minute, and savor.

1. Beautiful rosemary flowers. Unlike most herbs, their appearance generally does not change the taste of the herb for the worse.

2. If you garden outside of a city below Zone 7 (or anywhere below Zone 6), grow your rosemary in a big pot and bring it indoors for the winter.

3. Look for Christmas tree-shaped plants in stores around the holidays. Decorate, harvest sparingly, and then plant in the garden come spring.

sage

Won't make you *sage*; that's rosemary's job. This herb's Latin name means "to save," as in "salvation." Sage—generally dried and burned—has a long history of being used to cleanse away evil spirits. (As does unrelated sagebrush.) It may chase away evil gardening spirits as well. Some of the nonedible varieties give off so strong a camphorish scent that gardeners position them near caterpillar and borer-prone plants in hopes that they will function like natural mothballs (real ones being much too toxic for any home or garden) and repel the adult moths whose children cause the problem. Despite having "sage" in their common names, these strongly scented plants are technically salvias—"All sage are salvias, but not all salvias are sage."

SCIENTIFIC NAMES AND TYPES: Basic garden (common) sage is the essential stuffing herb *Salvia officinalis;* blue-flowered, a variety of multicolored leaf types have been developed, some of which are quite garish-looking and foul-tasting; the basic form (sometimes called green sage) is the best for cooking. *Salvias* are a huge family (actually a subfamily—they are technically mints), with close to 1,000 members, many of which have "sage" in their common names. Their range of flowers includes just about every conceivable color. *S. elegans* lives up to its name—the scent of this aptly named pineapple sage *is* elegant, as are its lipstick-red flowers. Both the leaves and the flowers are deliciously edible. You would not enjoy the leaves of *S. apiana* (white sage; bee sage), but its flowers (white to light blue) strongly attract pollinators (*apiana* = bees). And its heavily scented leaves make it the sage of choice for burning in small clumps to "smudge" a room clear of evil spirits and negativity, and in large amounts to replace sagebrush in sweat-lodge cleansing ceremonies.

GROWING TIPS: Basic garden sage should survive for several years in Northern gardens; most of the others are perennial only in much warmer climes. Starting from seed can be difficult and time-consuming; better to begin with plants or cuttings—they root easily.

HARVEST: Pick leaves for culinary use before the plant flowers.

BUYING: By scent; smell them!

STORAGE: Store fresh cuttings standing in water in the fridge. Sage dries wonderfully.

TRICKS: Allow pineapple sage to flower; the red blooms are a favorite of hummingbirds. Harvest a large batch of branches from any variety, dry, and place on a campfire or toss into a fireplace for herbal "salvation."

1. Common ("garden") sage. The most ordinary looking will be the best-tasting.

2. A very variegated sage indeed!

3. The elegant flowers of pineapple sage are a wonderful hummingbird lure.

Opposite page: A tricolor sage.

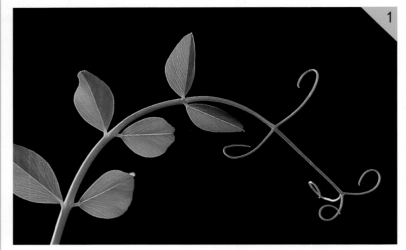

Delicate in appearance, yet amazingly cold-hardy. Extremely sweet, yet crunchy as a pretzel. Delicious cooked or raw, these little beauties are unsurpassed at brightening up stir-fry dishes. But fresh eating is where they really shine—try them atop springtime salads—if you can keep from eating them all right off the vine. Like a fine Beaujolais nouveau, snow peas predict the merits of the entire season to come.

SCIENTIFIC NAME: *Pisum sativum*

TYPES: Snow peas actually *are* a type of pea. They are just too special to share a page with shelling and snap peas. An improvement on snaps, there is no "string" to pull; every inch of the flattened pod is as sweet as the "fruit" of the most sugary shelling pea. Varieties with Oregon in the name (Oregon Sugar Pod, Oregon Giant) are the standard, bred by the maestro of peas, Dr. James Baggett of Oregon State University. But if you are growing them in the South (or anywhere spring is short), go for the variety with the shortest days to maturity—like Dwarf White Sugar or Short n' Sweet; both begin producing peas just 50 days after their seed is sown. Some varieties have beautiful purple flowers; look for this trait in catalogue descriptions.

GROWING TIPS: Same as for regular peas.

HARVEST: As soon as you see the little peas begin to swell inside the pods. Snow peas are at their best when still small, so do not let them linger on the vine. Search carefully; the pods blend in well with the foliage.

BUYING: Look for crispness and small pods. Reject any with overly large bulges.

STORAGE: In the fridge, in a vented plastic container, and use them quickly. Snow peas also freeze well. The traditional method is to blanch the pods in boiling water for one minute, quickly plunge into ice water, pat or spin dry, and then quickly freeze for winter stir-fry use. But some say that the pods will stay *salad* crisp if you freeze them promptly inside a block of ice!

TRICKS: Pods that stay undiscovered long enough to grow large with bulging peas are useless as "pod-and-all" food, and the last runs of the season tend to have very tough pods no matter what their size. But the peas inside will still be supersweet. Harvest these oversize monsters, zip them open like shelling peas, and enjoy the pearls inside. Or dry and save them for planting in the fall—those big peas *are* the seeds.

1. Few plants are more attractive than snow peas.

2. The flowers of many varieties are a lovely purple color; look for this trait when you purchase your seeds.

3. Do not let the bulging seeds inside the pods get as large as the largest of these before picking; you want pods with little bumps—not big marbles.

Opposite page: Plant your snow peas where they will catch the light of the morning sun through their translucent-when-young pods.

If the days are too hot or too long, *any* spinach will quickly go to seed. Even the seed refuses to sprout when the soil temperature gets even a bit too warm (70° is ideal). But in spring and fall—and even over winter in many areas—spinach will be very, very happy in your garden.

SCIENTIFIC NAME: *Spinacia oleracea*

TYPES: Smooth-leafed types are much easier to clean, but the plants are not as cold-tolerant (many "smoothies" are light-green, sweet Asian varieties with "Imperial" in their names). The leaves of savoy types—like those of *the* classic spinach variety Bloomsdale Longstanding—are very wrinkled and puckered-looking ("savoyed"), making them a real chore to clean—but the plants are so cold hardy they can be under snow for a week and not mind one bit. Semi-savoy types are in-between—both ways; the classic varieties Melody and Tyee fall into this category. Check catalogue descriptions carefully and choose varieties described as upright (as opposed to sprawling); they are much easier to pick and clean, no matter the leaf type.

GROWING TIPS: In spring, plant seeds as soon as the ground warms up (or put transplants out as soon as it thaws). In fall, "walk around your garden three times; if you have sweat on your brow, it's still too warm to plant spinach." Plant successive runs every two weeks both spring and fall for a continuous supply. In all but the far North, make a last fall sowing (of a cold-tolerant Savoy variety) two weeks to a month before frost, and mulch the young plants well with shredded leaves or protect them with floating row covers—they will provide your first eating come spring. In the Deep South, you should be able to harvest delicious leaves all winter long.

HARVEST: With scissors, cut-and-come-again style while the leaves are still small. Several more runs of leaves will regrow from the inch-tall stumps you leave behind.

BUYING: Look for rounded rather than pointy leaves (often a sign that the plants were getting ready to bolt). Small leaves are always best.

STORAGE: In the fridge, in open plastic bags lined with paper towels to absorb moisture.

TRICKS: When spring-sown spinach finally does bolt, allow the central stalk to develop and flower on a few plants, then pull up at the end of summer and shake the dried seed heads over a freshly prepared bed to self-sow your first fall crop.

1. The more puckered (savoyed) the leaves, the more cold-hardy—and hard to clean.

2. Smooth-leaved varieties are easy to wash, but the plants do not like really cold weather.

3. A perfect stand of spinach can outshine a patch of pretty posies.

Opposite page: Harvest the last run of spinach this way, rather than cut-and-come-again style. Snip off the roots and place the plants in a tall jar of water in the fridge. They will stay fresh a long time.

Even those with no outdoor space—or even a sunny windowsill—can grow their own food when they raise sprouts; and by so doing, consume the essence of the plant in question.

SCIENTIFIC NAMES AND TYPES: The two most commonly sprouted seeds are those of classic bean sprouts (the "Oriental" mung bean *Vigna radiata*; the seeds of all 150 species of the leguminous bean family *Vigna* are edible) and alfalfa sprouts (*Medicago sativa*—also a legume, this member of the edible pea family produces the ubiquitous health food store sprouts). But you can safely sprout the untreated seed of pretty much any edible. Especially tasty are broccoli and kale (mildly spicy), radishes and mustards (very spicy), cauliflower (peppery), sunflower (nutty), wheat (sweet and malty, which only makes sense, as dried grain sprouts *are* malt), and fennel (yes, licoricey).

GROWING TIPS: Place your seeds—always untreated and preferably organically grown—into a sterilized glass jar, and rinse several times, keeping the final rinse water in the jar. Set the jar aside for a few hours, then secure cheesecloth (or fresh, unused nylon window screening, which drains better) over the opening with a rubber band, pour out all the water and store the jar at room temperature in a draining position. Rinse the seeds well with fresh water at least twice a day—the more rinsing the better. Drain all water after rinsing. Sprouting time ranges from two to four days for mung beans and wheat to a week for alfalfa and sunflower seeds. Clever, somewhat automated sprouting devices like the three-level Bioset will do some of the work for you.

HARVEST: Within a day or two of the seeds' first sprouting.

BUYING: Look for bright color; sniff for off-flavor; check "sell by" dates.

STORAGE: In the fridge, in an open plastic bag that contains a paper towel to absorb excess moisture. Or replace the cloth of your sprouting jar with a real lid and refrigerate; many sprouts will continue to grow a bit this way.

TRICKS: Use the hose sprayer on your sink to wash the sprouts; it has just the right pressure. Your rinsing water should always be at room temperature; cold water will slow things down, while hot water can kill the plants or encourage mold. Treated seed is brightly dyed to reveal its chemical fungicide covering to farmers. *Never* sprout treated seeds.

1. Many seeds come packaged for sprouting; you can be sure these have not been treated with chemicals. Organically produced are the best choices.

2. Alfalfa sprouts in a sprouting device.

3. Red clover seeds come alive.

4. Devices like the Bioset allow you to sprout several types of seeds at the same time.

Opposite page: Mung beans (Chinese bean sprouts).

Store-bought berries can sometimes turn boring breakfast cereal into a life-enhancing experience. But even the best-tasting of those pales in comparison to the deeply floral, intense flavor of tiny alpine strawberries—and the only way to enjoy *those* is to grow your own.

SCIENTIFIC NAME: *Fragaria* species

TYPES: The kind of strawberry most often seen in supermarkets, Junebearer plants produce large berries over a period of just a few weeks. But that is not as limiting as it sounds; there are early-, mid-, and late-season varieties, which (despite their overall name) allow you to harvest from mid-spring through early summer when you plant all three types. Junebearer patches last many years with proper care. Day-neutral varieties produce all season long, but the berries are a bit smaller and the patch will not last as long; the farther North you are, the better these types will do. Both Junebearer and day-neutral types spread by aboveground runners. Alpines (which may or may not be exactly the same as the wood strawberry) grow from big clumps; the berries are small and pointy, intensely flavored, and appear from early spring through frost; a single plant will produce hundreds each season. They are sometimes called wild strawberries, and are not to be confused with the common weed, whose round "fruits" are inedible.

GROWING TIPS: Junebearers: Start with live plants (or rooted runners from a gardener refurbishing his or her patch), and cut your patch back to the ground every few years to reinvigorate the crowns. Strawberries in general prefer coolish climes; even Junebearers may need to be planted fresh each year in really torrid areas. Some day-neutral types and all alpines can be started from seed. Day-neutral patches tend to punk out after a few years and should be replaced. Alpines will go on forever if you thin out the old brown growth in spring and divide plants that have grown excessively large.

HARVEST: When fully colored and aromatic.

BUYING: By smell. Hold the vents of that plastic container right up to your nose and inhale deeply—if aroma is absent, the berries will be tasteless, no matter how good they look.

TRICKS: Strawberry pots keep the plants up nice and high, away from slugs and rot. Hanging baskets filled with alpines will be your first stop every time you step outside. (In the North, remove such plants from their containers and plant them in the garden over the winter.)

1. The distinctive leaves of strawberry plants.

2. First come flowers, then small green fruits . . .

3. . . .Then—finally, nice big berries.

4. Children may balk at pulling weeds, but few can resist the "chore" of picking ripe red berries.

5. A bucket full of berries—a good day's work.

Despite the hundreds of mislabeled signs you've read over the years, these members of the morning glory family are completely unrelated to yams. True yams (*Dioscorea alata*) are tropical giants whose underground roots look nothing like sweetpotatoes and take a full year to grow. Brown on the outside, white on the inside, yams are mostly water and starch, not at all sweet, and contain substances that closely resemble human hormones. (Yams were used to create the first birth control pills; the "wild yam" in women's natural health remedies comes from these plants.) Very few people in the United States have ever seen a true yam. But years ago, someone applied the nickname "the Louisiana yam" to a variety of sweetpotato named Beauregard—perhaps to appeal to early African Americans, who *were* familiar with the real thing. Sweetpotatoes have been misnamed yams ever since. True sweetpotatoes (one word; the official USDA spelling because they are also not potatoes of any kind) are much better-tasting—their succulent sugars replacing the yams' starch, and their neon red and orange colors heralding their nutrient-rich benefits. They are, in fact, one of the tastiest and most healthful things you can grow.

SCIENTIFIC NAME: *Ipomoea batatas*. (The common—and highly invasive—flowering vine we call morning glory is *Ipomoea indica*.)

GROWING TIPS: Take a full-size sweetpotato and bury it three-quarters down in moist sand or stick it butt-end in a jar of water; green shoots with exposed roots ("slips") will soon sprout out of the skin. Plant these outside when they have reached at least 6 inches high, after all danger of frost has passed. Vines will cover the soil. Then, after three or four months, your crop will await in the ground below.

HARVEST: Right *after* the first light frost.

BUYING: Good luck. The best sweetpotato looks pretty much like the worst one. Avoid visible rot.

STORAGE: Before you can store you must first "cure" the harvest—a mystical enterprise where you keep the tubers almost steaming (heat and humidity both in the 90s) for a week. Then place the cured tubers in a cool and dry place and they will last almost forever.

TRICKS: Although identified with the South, you *can* grow sweetpotatoes in the North. Choose a variety that produces tubers fairly quickly, start "slipping" the mother plant about two weeks before your last frost date, and think good thoughts.

1. A sweetpotato set in water to produce slips; toothpicks prevent the tuber from sinking all the way down.

2. A close look reveals the beauty of a slip.

The herb of happiness, strength, and courage. In cooking, the leaves help other spices achieve a full, complementary flavor. In natural healing, it is used as an antiseptic (its properties are well documented—the thymol listed as an ingredient in products such as mouthwash comes from thyme plants). Inhaling the steeping fumes is a centuries-old cure for congestion. In the garden, thyme's strong aroma is said to repel whiteflies. The flowers certainly do attract bees.

SCIENTIFIC NAMES AND TYPES: *Thymus vulgaris* is common garden thyme—the classic type used for cooking and natural medicine. *T. citriodorus* (sometimes presented as the *citriodorus* variety of wild thyme, *T. serpyllum*) is the sensational lemon-scented thyme; available in a variety of highly ornamental colorings (green-and-silver, green-and-gold, all yellow), the leaves' strong citrusy scent is highly valued in cooking and as a natural mosquito repellent. Both grow about a foot tall and will survive winter only in Zone 7 and warmer. Perennial anywhere is wild thyme itself *(T. serpyllum)*, known also as creeping thyme (which it really is not at 10 inches tall) and Mother of Thyme, it has nicely scented leaves, and despite its "wild" designation, many named ornamental varieties. *T. polytrichus* (sometimes *T. praecox*) is also known as wild or creeping thyme, and this one is a creeper—its extremely prostrate (only half-an-inch high) habit makes it an ideal groundcover with nicely fragrant leaves. Inch-high wooly thyme *(T. pseudolanuginosus* or *T. lanuginosus)* is an excellent groundcover type with ornamentally hairy leaves.

GROWING TIPS: Thyme is easy to start from seed, but with plants, you can sniff the leaves first and choose your variety by scent. Keep the soil a bit on the dry side and prune back mid-season if the plants get woody.

HARVEST: Pretty much anytime; this is an herb whose taste does not change after flowering.

BUYING: Choose by smell.

STORAGE: Dry or freeze.

TRICKS: Grow thyme in the center of your garden, so that bees will fly over (and visit) your other plants on their way in and out. University studies show that rubbing the crushed leaves of lemon-scented thyme on exposed skin repels mosquitoes just as well and almost as long as the chemical DEET, eclipsing all other natural—and many chemical—mosquito repellents.

1. A variegated type of thyme.

2. Stripping the leaves off common garden thyme, the choice for cooking and herbal antiseptic use.

3. A red-stemmed variety.

Opposite page: Golden thyme; one of many highly ornamental versions of the lemon-scented variety. Science has shown the crushed leaves of this citrus-scented herb to be a powerful natural mosquito repellent.

The garden favorite. Available in a mind-numbing number of varieties (enough to fuel several tomato-only seed catalogues), the fruits range from tiny little "grapes" to three-pound monsters, come in every color of the rainbow—including varieties that are green when ripe—and have names that promise wonderful stories with their provenance, like Jefferson Giant, Cherokee Purple, Arkansas Traveler, and German Johnson. Grow them for sauce, cooking the harvest down into a rich paste that allows you to eat "garden fresh" long after frost; for slicing as the perfect centerpiece of a BLT; or for "cherry picking," as you enjoy the seemingly endless cavalcade of tiny living candies those prolific plants produce. Or simply for the taste of that first ripe red one sampled in the field. But do grow these, the *true* fruits of summer!

SCIENTIFIC NAME: *Lycopersicon esculentum* ("wolf peach" in Greek).

TYPES: Cherry tomatoes are small, but—with few exceptions—grow on rampant vines that can become invasive. Paste, sauce, plum, or Roma (actually a specific variety name) plants produce medium-size, teardrop-shaped fruits prized for their abundant flesh and little juice. (Sandwich lovers note: Sliced "pasters" provide true tomato taste without the bread-soaking juice.) Medium-size round tomatoes are called slicers—despite the fact that the large, oblong beefsteak types (another variety name escaped to a full-blown class) are the type most often thought of for this use.

An important distinction for home growers is a variety's determinacy. Determinate types grow on fairly compact vines, produce one large flush of fruits, and are then done for the season; they are the best choice for limited garden space and container growing. Most paste tomatoes are determinate, and you will find more hybrid varieties in this category. Indeterminate tomatoes grow continuously all summer, producing their fruits in natural sequential fashion. Many indeterminate vines stretch 15 feet or more and require a great deal of space; almost all of the old heirloom varieties and cherries fall into this category, and most are open-pollinated types.

1. Purple Calabash; a deeply ribbed, dusky-colored heirloom variety that is extremely difficult to clean.

2. Paste tomatoes come in all sizes, like the extremely large Amish Giant and this similar variety, Cuban Paste.

3. Georgia Steak (aka Big Rainbow and many other names) is a large yellow beefsteak that develops a red dot at the blossom end that eventually "sunsets" beautifully through the entire fruit. Extremely sweet and low acid.

4. The unique flowers of the Wolf Peach.

FURTHER DISTINCTIONS: If you save the seed of an *open-pollinated* variety and plant it again the following season, you will get the same tomatoes. *Hybrid* varieties (by law always designated by "hybrid" or "F1" on plant markers and seed packets) are the result of intentionally crossing two different varieties to create a new tomato containing (one hopes) the best attributes of both parents. The saved seed of a hybrid will *not* produce the same fruits.

GROWING TIPS: Tomatoes are unique in that they grow auxiliary roots along any buried portion of their stem, giving the plant vastly increased access to food and water. Always bury at least half—preferably three-quarters—of the stalk when you plant. In cold climates, trench the buried part of the stem at a 90° angle, keeping it only an inch below the soil surface so that it stays in the warmest part of the soil. In warmer climes, bury it straight down, so that the roots are in the coolest dirt. Tomatoes are vines, and require support; continually securing the growing portion to a stake with cloth strips works well for compact, determinate varieties, but indeterminate beefsteak types do best inside a sturdy cage, which itself requires staking. Allow extra room between plants for airflow, remove discolored leaves promptly, and keep an inch of fresh compost on top of their soil to prevent disease.

HARVEST: Just before full ripeness occurs. The flavor of tomatoes comes largely from volatile aromatic oils, and just an extra day sitting in the sun will steal much of the taste.

BUYING: Avoid tomatoes that feel hard to the touch; half-ripe is fine if the colored-up areas give to gentle pressure.

STORAGE: *Never* in a refrigerator or on a sunny windowsill. Fruits should sit out in the open, away from direct sunlight, in single layers. Green and half-ripe ones will ripen at room temperature; or place in a paper bag with a ripe tomato, banana, or apple for faster results.

TRICKS: Place the dried, crushed shells of a dozen eggs in each hole when you plant; the calcium will prevent blossom-end rot and produce fruits with richer flavor.

1. Black Brandywine—the open-pollinated (*not* hybridized) result of breeding one of the black (very dark purple) Russian tomatoes with the classic pink beefsteak Brandywine, considered the best-tasting tomato of all time.

2. Brandy Boy *is* a hybrid—and its plants, filled with giant fruits, are a genuine improvement over the beloved heirloom, which often bears more like sweet corn than tomatoes (one or two "fruits" per plant).

3. A green Radiator Charlie's Mortgage Lifter; an heirloom tomato of prodigious size (typically over three pounds each) and story (there was this guy named Charlie who had a car repair shop down South during the Great Depression and sold these tomato plants . . .).

4. Many people feel that yellow tomatoes have lower acidity levels, but the difference is more in their sugar content— yellow tomatoes are generally much sweeter than reds.

5. Cherry tomatoes; grow them once and they will likely self-seed for you every season thereafter.

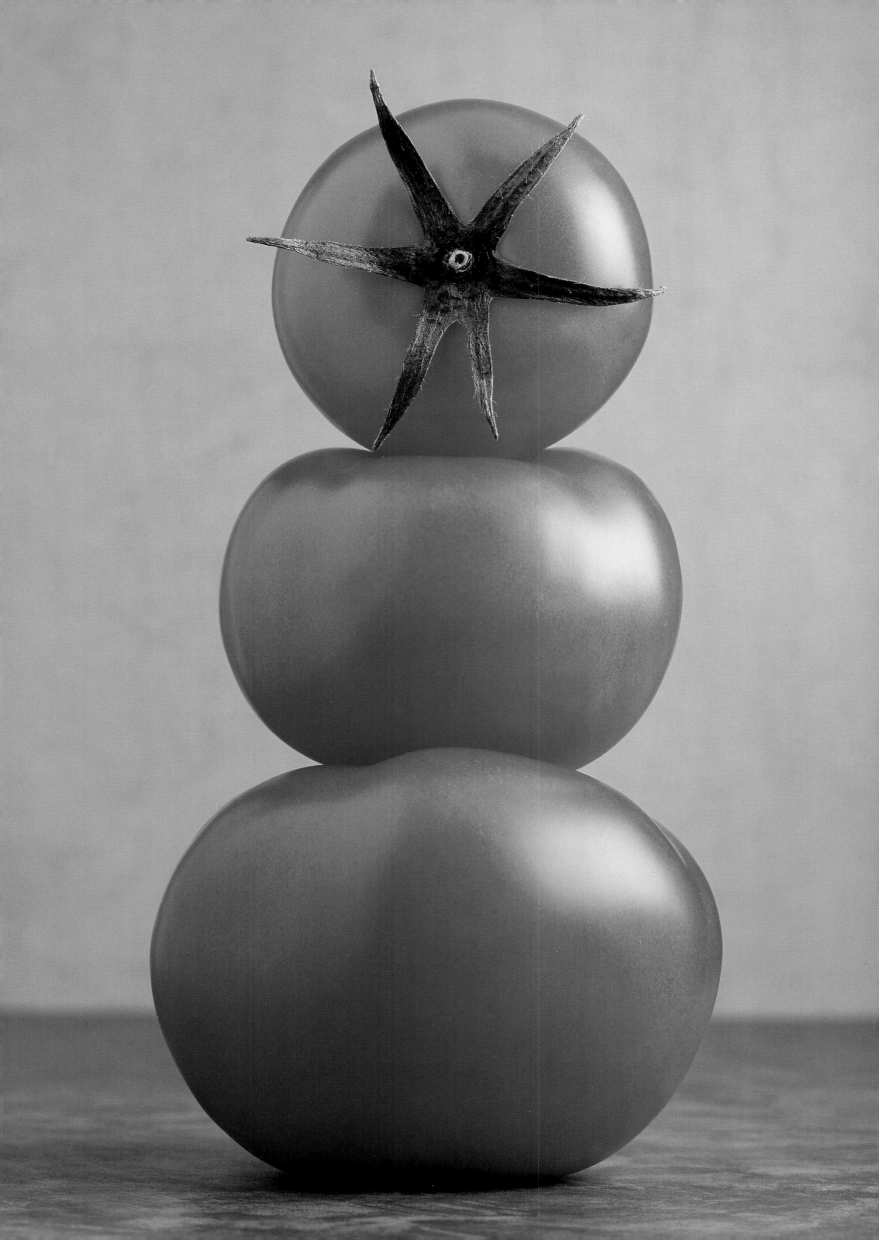

This cabbage family member was prized in every garden—essential to a family's winter survival—until it was upstaged by the arrival of the potato. Not the best choice of a replacement—turnips are rich in natural anticancer compounds and a great source of vitamin C. They are also much tastier (and prettier!) than most people realize—or will be, if you prepare them correctly. Enjoy them in winter soups—their natural role—but also try a few young and fresh from the garden. You will soon be finding new reasons to place them on your table.

SCIENTIFIC NAME: *Brassica rapa* (or *Brassica campestris*)

TYPES: Two basic root shapes (round and carrot-shaped) have been known since the fifth century. The flesh is always yellow or white, but the skin can be yellow, white, green, purple, or even "black." Fast-growing varieties (often indicated by "spring" in the name or description) are your best choice for small, young early roots and greens. Storage (or fall) types are planted in late summer for winter use. Some varieties are grown more for their abundance of nutritious greens than for the roots.

GROWING TIPS: Turnips are best sown early or late, not in-between. Spring crops are generally ready in a speedy 30 days (or pick the greens at two to three weeks old). Fall crops take about twice that long. Do not grow in midsummer; the roots will be tough and woody.

HARVEST: Quickly in spring; as with radishes, note the days to maturity on the seed packet and pick on time. For the tastiest *greens,* pull a week earlier (enjoy the roots as well—they are edible at any size). In fall, time your crop to be ready to pick right after the first light frost; that little chill will sweeten the roots.

BUYING: In spring, look for fresh greens on small roots. In fall, smaller is still better than large—larger versions of a single variety are the most likely to have begun getting tough.

STORAGE: In the fridge in spring. In fall, store the greens in the fridge and the roots in a cool, dark place.

1. Turnip greens are prized by those who know their nutritional value; in fact, you can sometimes find the greens alone—without the roots—in better produce markets.

2. Classic little white globes. The small, fresh leaves indicate that these roots will have the best flavor.

3. Should we be red or white? This pair of turnips could not decide.

Opposite page: Red-skinned turnips.

Nothing conjures up images of summer like a field full of juicy melons basking in the sunshine —sweet expectation on a vine.

SCIENTIFIC NAME: *Citrullus lanatus*

TYPES: The classic oblong types have a striped green rind and sweet red flesh. The flesh of the smallish, round, five-to-ten-pound icebox types may be red or yellow; these are easier to grow and often have the word "baby" in their name. There are also a large number of unusual varieties: dark yellow (almost orange) flesh; orange skin and red flesh; black skin with red or yellow flesh, etc. The classic heirloom variety Moon and Stars, a big, red-fleshed melon, is genetically disposed to having bright yellow celestial designs on both its skin and leaves.

GROWING TIPS: Watermelons like very warm soil, lots of sun, lots of water, and a nice long season to enjoy them in. In the North, choose smaller types and cover the ground with black plastic to trap heat; Blacktail Mountain, bred by noted heirloom enthusiast Glenn Drowns, is the fastest-ripening, cold-hardiest variety. In the South, take advantage of your longer season to grow the big classic types like Georgia Rattlesnake and Carolina Cross, which need at least three months of warm-weather growing and can reach 100 pounds or more when ripe.

HARVEST: There is nothing sadder than picking one a bit too early. And it is an easy mistake to make—ripeness-judging of watermelons is so difficult that professional pickers are paid extra if they possess the necessary divining skills. The best indicator of ripeness is the browning of the tendril closest to the fruit. Other clues include a color change (generally to yellow) where the melon touches the ground (the *couche,* or ground spot) and *loss* of gloss on the rind.

BUYING: No tendrils to help here; look for that colored ground spot and *un*glossy skin.

STORAGE: Watermelons keep their quality for two to three weeks at 60°. Chill *only* before serving; a watermelon will develop off-flavors after just a few days in the fridge.

TRICKS: Trellis the vines to save space; this works especially well with small, icebox varieties. You *can* grow your own seedless watermelons, but these varieties demand a very hot climate, and "normal" watermelons must be growing nearby for pollination.

1. Small, round icebox types are the best choice where the growing season is normal-to-short; look for the word "baby" in the variety name.

2. When dead ripe, the flesh of this Yellow Doll icebox type has a consistency and sweetly intense flavor more like that of a muskmelon.

3. Note the lush green tendril closest to this developing fruit. When that tendril loses its green color and withers to brown, the melon will likely be ripe.

4. Watermelon skins often sport artistic natural designs.

Winter squash are hard to beat for flavor, nutrition (all varieties are rich in beta-carotene), diversity, and good looks.

SCIENTIFIC NAMES AND TYPES: *Cucurbita maxima* includes many pumpkins and the hubbard, buttercup, kabocha ("Japanese"), and banana winter squashes; the best choice for Northern growers, they have the longest vines and biggest fruits. *C. moschata* includes more pumpkins (like the flattened heirloom Long Island Cheese, which may actually be a true winter squash) and the classic butternut squash; the longest-keeping types, their flavor improves the most in storage—and their solid stems keep vine borers at bay. *C. pepo* is a huge family that includes all the summer squashes and many pumpkins; its winter squash members—the acorn, spaghetti, Delicata, and dumpling types—tend to be the sweetest and grow on the best-behaved vines; they are best eaten fresh (before Christmas).

GROWING TIPS: Provide a rich soil, plenty of water, and do not rush the season. Despite its name, winter squash likes to grow in *very* warm temperatures—wait till several weeks after your last frost to plant.

HARVEST: Do not rush; you want the squash to be fully mature. On buttercups and kabochas, look for the stems to turn brown and corky. With other types, look for a fully ripe color (compare against photos from the seed pack or plant tag) and toughened-up skin—it should resist gentle pressure from your fingernail. Do not eat any of the types immediately—all winter squash taste much better a few weeks after picking.

BUYING: Use the fingernail test. Smaller squash do not necessarily taste better; if priced "by the each," take the largest one.

STORAGE: Simply let *C. pepo* varieties sit out in the open for a few weeks after harvest to cure. They can then be stored in a cool, dry place for two months, but will lose some flavor. Other types need to be cured in a hot, dry spot for a week—they can then be stored in cool and dry conditions for many months without any loss of flavor. In fact, most will sweeten up quite a bit as the months pass by.

1. Squash flowers precede the fruits. Like those of summer squash and pumpkins, the big blooms are delicious on their own.

2. The range of colors and shapes is enormous.

3. The highly ornamental Turk's Turban, an old European *C. pepo* variety, is grown mainly for decorative use but is also delicious when baked and stuffed.

Zucchini epitomizes the category of summer squash. The plants produce the most delicious edible blossoms of any food plant, and the flowers that escape such attention will quickly produce fruits that can (and should) be picked as soon as they are big enough *to* pick. The original baby vegetable, all varieties of summer squash should be enjoyed small and often. They taste best when they are young, and constant picking of fruits at just a few inches in size keeps the plants producing all season long. (This is also the best protection against having to deal with the gigantic tough, inedible baseball bats that are the inevitable result of being a bit on the slow side at picking time.)

SCIENTIFIC NAME: There are other squashes (acorn and pumpkin) in the *Cucurbita pepo* clan, but *all* summer squash are *C. pepo.*

TYPES: Yellow squash (which comes in straight and crook-necked shapes); pattypan (scallop) squash (mostly yellow; Peter Pan is green); and zucchinis—which come straight and round; green, yellow, or striped; and bushy (upright and well-behaved) or vining (Rampicante). The Lebanese types are pastel green, bulbous in shape, and said to be more prolific than zucchini!

GROWING TIPS: Largely easygoing, these hollow-stemmed squash have only one enormous pest problem—the squash vine borer. A moth that looks like a wasp lays eggs on the vine; those eggs hatch into "boring" larvae, which quickly tunnel inside the vine, weakening and often destroying the plant. Simply wiping the vine every other day with a damp cloth will destroy the eggs before they can hatch. Late plantings may not be affected. If you see a hole in the base of a vine with sawdust-like "frass" (bug poop) outside, slit open the vine, dispatch the nasty caterpillar-like thing inside, and heap your best soil over the injured area.

HARVEST: The smaller the better; a couple of inches across for the little scallops, four or five inches long for yellows and zukes—tops!

BUYING: Look for a bright, glossy skin and small size—the smaller the better.

STORAGE: Outside of abuse, it does not really seem to matter. Best enjoyed fresh, they seem to last equally long in the fridge or on a counter.

TRICKS: You do not have to choose between delicious edible squash blossom flowers and fabulous fruit. There is a golden moment when the baby fruits have *just* become big enough to eat and the flower is still attached and in good shape. Go for it!

1. A yellow summer squash.

2. Zucchini and other summer squash flowers are gourmet fare—especially when stuffed.

3. The classic green zucchini. Do not let them get any bigger than this.

Opposite page: A crookneck summer squash.

Acknowledgments

The author and photographer wish to extend their deepest gratitude to the lovely and talented Sharon Orlando.

We are indebted to many who supplied fresh edibles for the photographs in this book, most especially Jimmy Iovine of the legendary Iovine Brothers Produce in Philadelphia's Reading Terminal Market—a national treasure for food lovers.

Special thanks to Maryan Jaross; to Paul Stamets of Fungi Perfecti in Olympia, Washington, for the 'shrooms; and to all those who allowed us photographic access to their gardens: George Ball and Grace Romero of the famed W. Atlee Burpee Seed Company for entry to their trial and display gardens at historic Fordhook Farm; Derek Fell; Lynn Reynolds and landscape architect Carter van Dyke; James Day; Connie Deckman; Will and Gladys Grasse; Rebecca Grasse; Bob and Ray Lees; Bernice and Paul Rosenberg; Robin Rosenberger; Garren Teich; Jayne and Jacob of Wildemore Farm; Walt Yeutter; the good folks at Tarp Farm and at the Pennypack Farm CSA; and John W. Jordan, Virginia Trosino, and the members of Philadelphia's Sartain, South Street, and Waverly community gardens (sorry about the squash flowers).

Accolades to our lovely models, Cindy, Amanda, and Claire Smith.

Mike McGrath would like to acknowledge inspiration and information found in *The Plant Book* (Mynah, 2001); in the fine works of Sue Strickland and Kent Whealy (*Heirloom Vegetables,* Fireside Books, 1998); Roger Phillips and Martyn Rix (*The Random House Book of Vegetables,* 1993); William Woys Weaver (*Heirloom Vegetable Gardening,* Owl Books, 1997); Fearing Burr (*Field and Garden Vegetables of America,* American Botanist, 1988—a reprinting of the 1865 second edition); Anna Pavord (*The New Kitchen Garden,* DK, 1996); Dave DeWitt and Paul W. Bosland (*The Pepper Garden* and *Peppers of the World,* Ten Speed Press, 1993 and 1996, respectively); James Duke (*The Green Pharmacy,* Rodale, 1997); Andrew Chevalier (*The Encyclopedia of Medicinal Plants,* DK, 1996); Judith Benn Hurley (*The Good Herb,* Rodale, 1995); Amy Goldman (*Melons for the Passionate Grower,* Artisan, 2002); the *Johnny's Selected Seeds* catalogue; the writings and publications of J.I. and Robert Rodale; and the many talented writers, researchers, and editors who taught me so much during my years as Editor-in-Chief of *Organic Gardening* magazine: If I got something right, it's thanks to them; if I got it wrong, it's my fault.

And a big hand for our Abrams enablers: Esteemed editor Margaret L. Kaplan, the patient and persistent Jon Cipriaso, and distinctive designer Darilyn L. Carnes.

Tools and supplies were graciously provided by Lee Valley Tools of Ogdensburg, New York.

Editor:
Margaret L. Kaplan

Editorial Assistant:
Jon Cipriaso

Designer:
Darilyn Lowe Carnes

Production Manager:
Justine Keefe

Library of Congress Cataloging-in-Publication Data

McGrath, Michael, 1952–
  Kitchen garden A to Z : growing, harvesting, buying, storing / text by Michael McGrath ; photography by Gordon Smith.
    p. cm.
  Includes bibliographical references and index.
  ISBN 0–8109–5580–6 (hardcover)
  1. Kitchen gardens. 2. Vegetable gardening.
  3. Herb gardening. 4. Fruit culture.
  I. Smith, Gordon, 1950 Nov. 16– II. Title.

SB321M393 2004
635—dc22   2004004247

Text copyright © 2004 Mike McGrath
Photographs © 2004 Gordon Smith

Printed and bound in China

10 9 8 7 6 5 4 3 2 1

Harry N. Abrams, Inc.
100 Fifth Avenue
New York, N.Y. 10011
www.abramsbooks.com

Abrams is a subsidiary of LA MARTINIÈRE

Storage Basics at a Glance

See individual entries for more detailed information

ARTICHOKE	Refrigerate in plastic bags, freeze whole, or pickle.
ASPARAGUS	Refrigerate in plastic bags, pickle, or freeze puree.
BASIL	Keep at room temperature or refrigerate in plastic bags. Do not dry.
BEANS (fresh)	Refrigerate in open plastic bags, or pickle.
BEANS (dry)	Keep cool and dry in tightly lidded jars.
BEETS	Refrigerate greens in plastic bags. Keep roots cool and dry.
BLUEBERRIES	Refrigerate in vented hard plastic containers, or freeze.
BROCCOLI	Refrigerate in plastic bags; freeze or puree florets.
CABBAGE	Wrap in newspaper; keep cool, dark, and moist.
CARROTS	Remove tops. Keep in plastic bags in refrigerator or in cool sand.
CAULIFLOWER	Refrigerate in plastic bags, or freeze puree.
CELERY	Refrigerate in plastic bags or standing in water.
CORN (sweet)	Refrigerate instantly, unhusked.
CORN (dry)	Keep cool and dry, in tightly lidded jars.
CUCUMBERS	Keep at cool room temperature. Do not refrigerate.
DILL	Freeze or dry leaves. Dry seeds. Pickle both.
EGGPLANT	Keep at cool room temperature. Do not refrigerate.
ENDIVE	Refrigerate in plastic bags.
FENNEL	Refrigerate the bulbs in plastic bags, the leaves standing in water.
FLOWERS	Refrigerate loosely packed in lidded containers.
GARLIC	Keep cured heads at cool room temperature. Do not refrigerate.
JERUSALEM ARTICHOKES	Refrigerate in open plastic bags, or freeze.
KALE	Refrigerate in open plastic bags.
KOHLRABI	Refrigerate in the crisper section.
LEEKS	Remove roots, trim tops, and refrigerate.
LETTUCE	Pat or spin dry and refrigerate in open plastic bags.
MELONS	Refrigerate muskmelons. Keep honeydews cool and dry.
MESCLUN	Pat or spin dry and refrigerate in open plastic bags.
MINTS	Dry or freeze stripped leaves.
MUSHROOMS	Keep at cool room temperature.
MUSTARD GREENS	Refrigerate in open plastic bags.
ONIONS	Keep at high humidity (70 percent) and low (40°) temperature.
OREGANO	Dry or freeze stripped leaves.
PARSLEY	Refrigerate standing in an inch of water in a tall container.
PEAS	Freeze shelling peas. Refrigerate snaps in plastic bags.
PEPPERS (sweet)	Refrigerate in open plastic bags. Dry or freeze slices.
PEPPERS (hot)	Refrigerate in open plastic bags. Dry or make into sauce.
POTATOES	Keep in a dark, cool, dry spot, away from all light.
PUMPKINS	Keep in a cool (50–60°) dry spot.
RADISHES	Refrigerate spring radishes. Remove tops from fall radishes, refrigerate or keep in sand.
RASPBERRIES	Refrigerate in vented hard plastic containers, or freeze.
RHUBARB	Refrigerate in open plastic bags, or freeze chunks.
ROSEMARY	Refrigerate standing in a little water in a tall container.
SAGE	Refrigerate standing in a little water in a tall container, or dry.
SNOW PEAS	Refrigerate in vented hard plastic containers, or freeze.
SPINACH	Pat or spin dry and refrigerate in open plastic bags, or freeze puree.
SPROUTS	Refrigerate in an open plastic bag with a dry paper towel.
STRAWBERRIES	Refrigerate in vented hard plastic containers, or freeze slices.
SWEETPOTATOES	In a cool (50°) dry spot.
THYME	Dry or freeze.
TOMATOES	Keep at cool room temperature. Do not refrigerate.
TURNIPS	Refrigerate spring turnips. Remove tops from fall turnips, refrigerate or keep in sand.
WATERMELON	Keep at 60°. Do not refrigerate long-term; chill only before serving.
WINTER SQUASH	Keep in a cool dry place.
ZUCCHINI	Refrigerate or keep at room temperature.

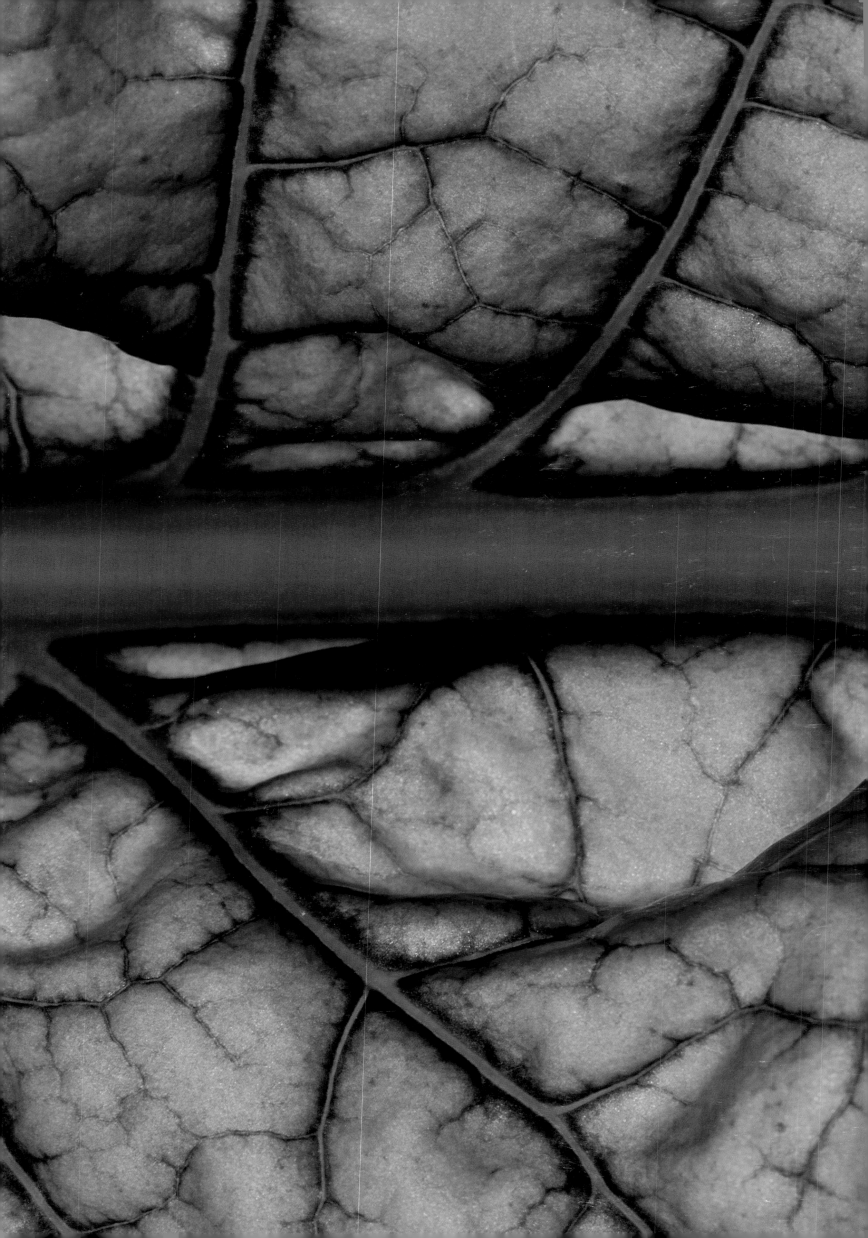